LOVING
YOURSELF

WITHOUT
LOSING
YOUR COOL™

LOVING YOURSELF
WITHOUT LOSING YOUR COOL™

SHANTELLE BISSON

YGTMedia Co. Trade Paperback Edition.
ISBN trade paperback: 978-1-989716-68-7
eBook: 978-1-989716-69-4
Audio book: 978-1-989716-70-0

Published in Canada, for Global Distribution by YGTMedia Co. www.ygtmedia.co/publishing
To order additional copies of this book: publishing@ygtmedia.co

Edited by Kelly Lamb
Interior design and typesetting by Doris Chung
Cover design by Michelle Fairbanks
ePub edition by Ellie Silpa
Shutterstock © popovartem.com

TORONTO

You don't need to be paralyzed by fear to still be stifled because of it.

This book is for all the women who lost themselves along the way on this wonderful, complicated journey called life.
Welcome home.
And to Caroline for getting it all before it was too late.
xx
Shantelle

I know you without actually knowing you at all. I know that somewhere inside of you—either buried deep down or simmering at the surface threatening to boil over at any moment—is your fear. Fear: an unpleasant often strong emotion caused by anticipation or awareness of danger. (*Merriam-Webster Dictionary*)

We all have it.

It's what keeps us up at night.

It's what keeps us playing small.

It's what keeps us in jobs, relationships, and towns we extract no joy or fulfillment from.

It's what keeps us from pursuing interests, passions, and dreams.

Fear is what has us living half a life. Punching our timecards through life without ever doing a single thing we had told ourselves as children we would try, we would accomplish, we would enjoy.

You don't have to be fully consumed by fear for it to have a foothold on the extent to which you're living your life out loud. You don't need to be paralyzed by fear to still be stifled because of it.

But if you are a living breathing human you are likely being corralled

In order to live a life worth living, we must be committed to being BRAVE. I've written this book to help you become brave.

by your fear. I am here to tell you that living with fear and unhealed shit is no way to live your one life. I know because I was doing it, and I was a total and utter mess. In order to live a life worth living, we must be committed to being BRAVE. I've written this book to help you become brave.

I believe in you! I know that you can do it!

And when you do, you will be so in love with yourself and your life that you won't be able to be stopped.

Here is a teeny tiny tip of the iceberg list of fears that might be driving your patterns of not loving yourself enough to go and get the life you know you want. Of not doing the work to heal the traumas so you can move the fuck on already and go live the life you've always desired. I've composed this list for you, because it's part of the list I fight through all the damn time in my pursuit of writing books, of sharing my stories with you. You see, fear does not discriminate based on gender, race, language, or socioeconomic status. Fear is readily available to stop us all dead in our tracks, and it might look a little something like this for you:

Fear of not being good enough. Fear of not being smart enough.

Fear that your dreams, your ideas, your passions are stupid, childish, and unworthy of pursuit.

Fear that you don't have enough experience to go after that promotion.

Fear that everybody will find out you're a fraud. (I struggle with this one A LOT!)

Fear that you aren't actually talented in your chosen field. (This is me every day as a writer, and back in the day when I was acting).

Fear that you won't be respected or taken seriously.

Fear that you are not loveable. Fear that you will get hurt.

Fear that you will fail. Fear that you are not worthy of a better life.

Fear that once you get a better life you will only destroy it, so why even bother.

Fear, fear, fear, fear, fear.

It is my dream for you that by the end of this book you will have healed so much of the bullshit that has taken up residency in your spirit that you will conquer your fears and go after loving yourself more wholly. That you won't live a life out loud void of fears, but that you will live it wholly in spite of them.

I'm honored and proud to be on this journey with you. Let's do THIS!

Over the many, many years of my healing journey, I've found the most impactful, lasting change came once I began to add journaling to all my other inner work. Prior to the addition of the journaling component, it seemed that the work was just a collection of words, advice, and recommendations floating around in my head. I "got" what therapists and coaches were telling me about what I needed to do to heal, let go, move on, forgive, all the things . . . but without me actually making the physical connection between the advice and my internal work, I found that nothing actually stuck. Somewhere along the way, I was given the advice to connect the dots and journal in tandem with all the other emotional and mental healing work I was doing. I was dubious to say the least, since so much of my inner work had only gone so deep. Now I'm sharing with you what I believe was the one-two punch needed to really bring my healing across the finish line. Which is why this book comes highly recommended with the blank *Without Losing Your Cool* (*WLYC*) journal. It's not enough to just read this book. It's not enough to just think about making the changes, or to simply intellectualize the reflective exercises you are going to encounter through the entirety of this book. You have to make the mental, emotional, and physical connection of it all, and the ideal way to do that is to ensure you journal when my book calls you to. And there's no better way to do that than with your own *WLYC* accompaniment journal. Feel free to order it now . . . or start in your own journal, whatever you have at your fingertips to get this healing party started!

OF MY OWN
ADMISSION

How I landed here

The first time I felt like I hated myself, I remember it like it was yesterday. When I close my eyes, I can see and relive the moment like it's happening in real time.

My formative years were spent in a low-rise apartment complex. There were two buildings, each comprising five floors, with not a lot of units between the two. I think there were twelve or fourteen on every single floor. And there were lots of kids. There was a pretty good gang of us running around, all super close in age. There were two playgrounds, one directly below my apartment on the third floor, and another in a field beside the pool. While our parents were at full-time jobs, we congregated for hours and hours on hot summer days, playing "Red Rover" and "Mother, May I" in the fields, while we waited for the pool to open at 1 p.m. In the winter months, we had our garages (if you were lucky enough to have one) to hang out in, and a hill—that back when I was six until twelve—felt like the biggest toboggan hill ever! (I have since revisited it, and surprise, surprise, it's not large, like at all! A child's perspective, am I right?!) We all played together day in day out, girls and boys enjoying being little and having some autotomy in what felt like a utopian world.

I say felt like because what did I know back then? I didn't know that girls didn't share a room with their mom or that not everybody had an adult roommate living in their three-bedroom apartment. And I sure as shit didn't know about sex or alcoholic and abusive runaround men. I remember being extremely happy. Sharing not only a room but a bed with my mom made me feel safe—and special. Like I had her all to myself, and I loved that. I also didn't know that our apartment pool was actually not much larger than pools that some people had in their own backyards. I was blissfully unaware, living my best little kid life.

Until one day when my breasts began to sprout.

I was nine.

Hair began popping up in places it hadn't been before.

I felt weird, it seemed weird, but my mom did her best to assure me that it was all "normal." It was extremely *early*, but normal; I decided to trust her.

So, I carried on, developing, and still trying to be a little girl. And I did so quite successfully, until the boys who used to play tag with me and race me in the pool, who were meant to be playing with my older brother, began hiding in my bedroom closet. They spied on my naked body, and jumped out of said closet to catch a glimpse of "developing" me without any clothes on.

This was the first time I vividly recall feeling scared. Alone. And angry. Very angry, in fact, but surprisingly, not at the boys with the extremely bad behavior or my older brother for not protecting me. But mad at my body.

It was on that day that I began to be angry at my body for betraying me. For changing in a way that no longer kept me safe. For being the vessel of six years of sexual abuse, rape, and trauma that would pave the way for how I would view myself in the world. The actions that "my friends" did on a regular basis, actions that some parents might dismiss as "boys just being boys," shaped the woman I would become.

A woman who was sure that all the male gender ever wanted was sex. And if you wouldn't give it to them, they would simply take it.

A woman who was sure that sex was what every single man I encountered wanted from me.

A woman who had nothing but her body and her looks to offer to men.

A woman who was not safe. Not safe in her own home—alone or with family members.

A woman who was not safe in the homes of others.

A woman who often still sleeps with the lights on when all alone.

A woman who always owns at least one big dog.

A woman who gets asked over and over again, "Why can't you be alone in a dark home at night without feeling fear?"

How do you feel "safe" in your home when almost every single sexual trauma that was committed against you happened in your home? I have news for you—you don't. Or at least not easily.

A woman who didn't fully trust that the man who fell in love with her, would love her unconditionally. Or that he wouldn't love her with cellulite or a flabby stomach or with saggy tits. And so began a lifetime of carving herself up to make sure she always stayed attractive to him and for him.

A woman who thought the only good in her was this body that so many men seemed hell-bent and determined to "own," to "have," and to "ruin."

When I was eighteen, I once had a date with the son of one of my mother's superiors, who took me to dinner, then to a dark deserted road. He pulled over and started to kiss me aggressively and tried to straddle me in the passenger seat. I told him if he didn't stop immediately and take me home, I would tell my mother what he did to me, and she in turn would have to tell his father.

He took me home.

I got called names during my entire high school experience. Even family members had things to say about how many guys I "went through" because, well, I never told anyone, not even my mother, what her superior's son had tried to do to me on that date. And I never told my mom that I was raped by a family member when I was eleven. I also didn't immediately tell my mother about my step-grandfather's groping and sexually perverted dialogue he would spew at me the second I was alone at a family gathering. So, it always just looked like boys asked me out, I would go, then I would promptly stop seeing them. Or at least just the ones who tried to take from me something that was not theirs to have.

In protecting myself, at long last, I was somehow made out to be the villain. I was called a "barracuda." I was the bad guy for not giving the wrong men the chance to hurt me.

I've been asked time and time again, why I didn't let my mother in on what I had endured during those six years. And to me the reason was clear cut. I never told her because when she wasn't being a young single mother, she was dealing with an alcoholic, abusive runaround of a husband. To say she had enough on her plate to cope with would have been an understatement.

There was another reason why I never told her. And this was likely the one that would do the most internal damage to me. The other reason I didn't share what was being done to me with her was because, I mean, after all, it must have been my fault. I must have had everything to do with why these things happened to me over and over and over again. It had to be me, and the filthy body that I had developed.

It surely had to be my body. It had to be me why other women hated me . . . to the point where they would write "slut" on my locker. Pour coke inside of it. And they made some sort of sick pact with each other that when they graduated, they would call me out as their pet peeve.

You see, I've spent the lion's share of my entire lifetime disconnected from me. My value. My worth. My essence.

And all I had simply done was be born. Exist. A child of God. Vibrant. Joyful. Trusting.

Fighting to protect myself from an age when I should have still been blissfully playing with dolls.

I don't recall a great deal about my childhood, but what I do recall is wishing for the safety of a father once the sexual abuse started to happen. I vividly remember lying in my bed one night after another closet attack, crying, wishing that my dad would be my hero. Wishing that my brother had never let his friends assault me. That's when I recall starting to feel real anger.

Anger that when my father finally did return to my life, he did what all the other men in my life seemed to be doing to me: take advantage of me. Use me. Hurt me. The father I wanted nothing more than love and protection from came back into my life and cleaned out my bank account. I was a child model, at his persistent pestering of my mother. She didn't want that for me at all, but my dad did. And he wouldn't quit until my mother finally caved. He was persuasive, even got me on his side, encouraging me to want it, telling me tales of how beautiful I was, how much money I could make. I didn't care about any of that. What I did care about more than anything in the world was that my father, who had never really given me the time of day, finally loved me. He was finally interested in me. He saw some value in me. He believed in me. He cared about me. And maybe, just maybe, if he ended up loving and caring for me, he would also protect me. Because up until that point, he'd literally wanted nothing to do with me. My brothers were his pride and joy; they had hockey, they were male, and they had his attention and what looked like to me as a young child, his love, which I desperately wanted. What I didn't know then as a young girl was that my father was a master manipulator, and what I internalized as receiving love from him was actually him working his master plan over me. Get me modeling and making money, so he could take it.

All of it.

He took all my money.

I was a little girl trying to be loved by her father, and I got played. It stung like a son of a bitch when I turned eleven and asked my mom if I could use my money to buy something special for myself. It was then that she had to tell me that my father had taken it all. I never addressed it with him. What do you say to a man who's willing to pimp his own daughter and take all her money?

Nothing.

You say nothing.

I spent until seventeen trying to fully win him over. The final straw for me wasn't when he completely ignored/forgot my sweet sixteen, but it was when he invited me as his guest to a polo match that he'd been invited to by some bigwig clients. I drove all the way north of Toronto to meet him there. I thought we were going to have a lovely father–daughter day together, but what happened instead broke my heart . . . again. My dad paraded me around, trying to convince people that I was his daughter, grinning like the cat who caught the canary any time a wealthy, more successful male declared their disbelief that there was no way a man like him could have produced a daughter like me. It was embarrassing, and I did the best I could to be polite, smile, and take it on the chin.

The kicker was when he reported back to my mother that I had humiliated him, walking around the event like I owned the place. Another lie. Another betrayal from a man who all I wanted was his love.

And again, the anger turned inward.

What was wrong with me? Why did men keep doing these awful things to me?

Why did they jump out of my closet to gawk at me naked?

Why did they fondle me in dark corners when we were all alone?

Why was I raped by a family member when I was only eleven?

Why did a group of them break into my house and attempt to rape me soon after I was raped? Was it the way I walked? Did they know that somebody else had already had sex with me? Why a couple short months later did they come to my home and try to do the same?

Why did a step-grandfather say heinous, sexual things to me while my entire family was gathered around?

Why did older boys try to have sex with me in ninth grade?

Why did older girls call me a slut, even though I still had never had consensual sex with anybody?

Why did my body do this to me?

And so began my journey of a lifetime of self-hate that started with self-harm at fifteen, and bulimia at seventeen when my high school boyfriend—the only one I actually ended up having sex with—broke up with me because of my "thunder thighs." Up until he said that, I hadn't actually ever paid any attention to the weight my body was. I had only ever been thankful for her ability to allow me to dance four days a week, because dance was my escape. Dance was my joy. Dance gave me a reason to love my body for something other than how others perceived her.

That was until the legs I had always thought of as strong, capable, and my salvation were called fat, ugly, and awful.

It was that day that I began to not only emotionally hate myself and my body, but physically as well. She was never ever good enough ever again. It was this exact moment in time that I began a lifetime of trying to starve, carve, and beat her into something better.

Something worthy.

Something loveable.

And I have news for every single one of you who picked up this book, who may have a similar life journey to self-hate as me: none of the external attempts to make myself loveable worked. No matter how many tens of thousands I spent on plastic surgery. No matter how many hours spent in the gym. No matter if the scale said 118 or 168, my level of radical self-love and acceptance never came.

I'd been deeply, painfully mad at my body for forty-three years.

An entire lifetime.

Almost over. Almost wasted. Until now. When I turned fifty-two and turned the page.

I refuse to loathe or live outside myself any longer.

I refuse to buy the tale that I'm unworthy.

And so now I give you this book. These tools. My words of how to love yourself without losing your cool in the hopes that you, like me, will spend the rest of the days of your life loving yourself—unapologetically and without regret or explanation to anybody else—exactly as you are. You don't even need to have the same wild ride I've been on as your life experience. Or your life journey might even be a thousand times more heinous, traumatic, and horrible. Whatever your story is, I'm here as your mirror that if I can get to the other side of all this fucking muck without completely crashing and burning, of spending a life addicted to drugs, alcohol, or both, then you can too. You, too, can rise above the darkness of others who would have crushed you, who would have "ended" you, who would have destroyed you, and you can end up living your best, most beautiful, most blessed ONE LIFE.

You hold the power of your todays and your tomorrows. You do. And only you. I'm going to help you reclaim your inner badass, the same way I reclaimed mine.

THE WHY

Why did I write this book?
What is its purpose?

I'm famous for saying, "being a woman is truly the hardest job in the entire world." But even though I believe this to be 1,000 percent true, there is no way in hell, like never ever, could you pay me or persuade me to come back in my next life as a man. Because even though being a woman is literally the most difficult thing to be, I'd still rather be a woman over anything else. Even on my worst days, I love being female. I love having the power to create life. I love participating in that miracle. I love that as a mother, my three daughters turn to me for all things. We have that unbreakable bond. I love that we are healers. That we are the fiber, the core, the strength of not only our families, but our society as a whole. I love that being female gives us incredible freedoms, liberties, and power that no man will ever know. We are free in all the most beautiful, important, and meaningful ways.

Is there much work for our equality in our modern world? Hell, yes.

Are we still oppressed in many, far too many, cultures? Also, sadly, yes.

But even with all the outwardly seeming negative aspects to being female, it still is a tremendous blessing to have the power, the privilege, and the gift of being one.

We as women have tremendous strength, like that of a lioness capable of fending for herself, and the ability to, alone, teach her children every single thing they will ever need to know about life.

We are formidable.

We are nurturing.

We are fierce.

We are soft.

We are powerful.

We are all these things, yet somehow, we are also grossly underpaid and overextended in every single area of our lives. In romantic relationships, we often lose ourselves almost instantaneously, taking over cooking, cleaning, supporting, and championing our lovers. We are sometimes abused by men we're trying to convince to love us. In our friendships, we often stay too long out of fear of hurting them by calling it. If we choose to become mothers, we might leave fulfilling careers to stay home to raise our children, to be hands on. Or we might head back into the workforce, while making sure we still get home in time to put dinner on the table and to nurture and care for an entire household, often missing precious life moments with our children that we can never get back and beating ourselves up with guilt over the need and desire to be a whole human. I've been both moms. I've been the one with a passion in her heart to fulfill ambitions while I was young enough to still go after them, and I've been the full-time stay-at-home mother. And I can say without a doubt that I've experienced "mom guilt" in both instances for all the reasons you likely have too.

Perhaps you're a female who has opted for none of these things. Maybe you favor a lover rather than a full-time partner because, let's be honest, those full-time partners are a whole whack of work, and sometimes not always worth the energy. No offense, but often having an intimate relationship is like having another child. Somebody else to emotionally and physically support. There are days, long days, that often roll from one into another when nobody has stopped to ask, "How are you doing?"

Sometimes you're so in the cycle of doing, caring, and managing that it's been days, weeks, perhaps even months since you stopped and asked yourself the exact same question.

Whatever kind of woman you are, I'm here to tell you that no matter how different our paths are, no matter our socioeconomic differences, our race, our religion, if you've had childhood, teen, or adult trauma, I would lay my last dollar on the fact that we all have these two things in common: 1) We've all put ourselves aside. In many cases to the point of neglect, where we don't take care of ourselves at all. 2) We've hated our bodies for at least part of our lives. And our common hatred has likely manifested in allowing partners to control what we do, how we look, the sort of sex we will have with somebody, and in extreme cases, withholding food from our bodies to force it to look a certain way.

You might be ready to toss this book back down on the shelf you picked it up from because you're thinking: "This isn't me. I'm not a victim, not a sexual abuse survivor. My dad wasn't an alcoholic. My parents were and are still together. I don't neglect myself. I get my hair done every six weeks, I get a mani/pedi twice a month, and I even work out four to six times a week. You don't know shit about shit. I totally do not neglect myself. And I definitely don't hate myself either. In fact, I know I'm extremely awesome, and I love my self completely."

Okay, cool. You're one of the extremely fortunate ones. You've gotten through life scot-free with loving parents and perhaps even a healthy partnership. You got the outward taking care of yourself down pat. Well done, you. I'm not out here trying to manifest difficulties in your life that don't exist. I'm also not trying to cause you to create drama, upset, or trauma so you can relate to this book. In fact, I dare say as a woman, you don't even need to have had as chaotic a childhood that I've had to be able to appreciate this reality: if you are female, you are cutting corners on your self-love and self-care, somewhere.

And I'm about to help you find those corners that you're cutting on yourself.

Help you really show up for yourself every single day, even on the days you don't want to or don't have the will to. We're going to talk about what showing up 100 percent looks like, ESPECIALLY ON THOSE DAYS.

I'm not talking about the surface prioritizing of you, I'm talking about the deep down, soul level, heart soothing self-love nurturing of YOU.

How deep into that are you? How well are you taking care of all the corners of yourself, those hard to reach way in the back self-love crevices?

I'm probing here because as a woman who got with her man at eighteen and had my first baby at nineteen, I literally had no fucking clue what taking care of me looked like. I mean, how could I? I was nineteen, a sexual abuse survivor, and now a young mom. Most nineteen-year-olds are changing their majors at university instead of changing diapers at home, am I right?! Looking after me and what I wanted didn't come into play until I turned thirty-four and realized that the marriage I was in, the relationship I had built as a teen, was not only not working right then and there, it sure as shit wasn't going to work for me for the rest of my life. Not in the state it was in.

It wasn't what I wanted (or so I thought). I say "I thought" because after an almost one-year hiatus on our marriage, where we both dated other people, I came to realize when I would lie alone in my bed at night and do visualization exercises, the hand that was holding mine on walks along the beach in Italy in my fifties (which I am now fucking in! Holy hell! That happened quickly . . . but I digress!) was Yannick. It was always his hand. His face. His voice. His laugh. So, I had to figure it out. I had to get to the bottom of what was really going on. Uncover why I was angry at never having figured out who I was and what I wanted. Put to rest the blame game I was playing in my mind with my husband. Why I was hell-bent on making him pay for all the shit, all the crimes that the

If you want
to live a full,
rich, healthy
life, YOU
need to
make that
happen.

other men in my life had committed against me. I needed to get to the root of why contentment, joy, and peace eluded me.

I had to stop dicking around and finally make the commitment to heal all the trauma and abuse, sexual and emotional, I had endured from, well, essentially the womb.

Because the reality was—and continues to be for not only me but you as well—that there ain't no knight in shining armor. Nobody, and I mean NOBODY, not even your partner of sixteen years who loves you (as was the case of my husband at the time of my complete breakdown) is coming to save you. Nobody is going to fucking save you.

If you want to live a full, rich, healthy life, YOU need to make that happen.

YOU need to decide to heal.

YOU need to do the work.

YOU and only YOU can heal you. Only you can give you the life you desire. Nobody is coming to do the work for you. This isn't somebody else's job; it is your job. You aren't anybody's project; you are your own project. Stop waiting. Stop making excuses. And start creating your plan. With me.

Even though I thought my marriage and being a mom were responsible for my unhappiness, I was able to legitimately uncover the truth during my one-year separation that I, and I alone, was responsible for my own unhappiness. And I am confident I can help you uncover yours.

Did my marriage have huge issues and cracks? Was there healing that needed to take place? ABSOLUTELY. There had been infidelity. There had been verbal abuse. There had been so much hurt, distrust, anger, and disappointment. There was a lot of mess to clean up. We were eighteen when we got together. I was a sexual abuse survivor that only a couple of people knew about, and not one of those two people was the man I was in an intimate relationship with. How well could that work out? Let me tell you, not well at all. Nothing like punishing somebody for a crime they not only did not commit, they didn't even know anything about it.

Healthy? Not one bit.

It was a miracle that we made it as far as we did.

But this book isn't about my marriage and all the healing that took place in it; that will be its own book, you can mark my words. This book is about getting to that place in your life where you stop holding the wrong people for ransom. This book is to ensure that you no longer misplace your anger, your pain, your disappointment on the shoulders of people who actually love you. Who are in your corner. This book is a guide to help you love yourself wholly.

To slay your demons.

To heal your past.

To release your expectations.

To stand in your power.

To live your best one life.

My journey to healing was lengthy, complex, and involved. But I did it. I got the job done. I arrived to that place where I now live my life in peace. Not in perfection, since we all know there is no such thing, but in peace. The peace of knowing that none of the things that happened to me were my fault. The peace of understanding that how somebody treats you says everything you need to know about them and nothing at all about you. Can I get an AMEN?!

And while I type this, I also want to point out that the issues in our relationships (work, friendships, or intimate) cannot be placed squarely on the shoulders of everybody ELSE in our lives. Me saying that the way somebody treats you says more about them and nothing at all about you is not the same thing as you getting a "get out of jail free card" to be a piece of shit in your own relationships. Let's not get confused here. Okay? Because that's not at all what I'm saying. Some of us (who shall remain nameless, like moi) find it very easy to spin a scenario to the point where none of the people involved, save for me, knows which end is up. This deflection skill of mine was absolutely developed as part of my survival tool kit. Sort of like the "shoot first" mentality, if you know what I mean.

Sometimes when I look back on my life and all the shit that came at me, I honestly wonder how I didn't end up addicted to drugs or alcohol, which is so rampant on my paternal side. How I didn't end up as a statistic. Rather than becoming a number on a chart, I instead have two thriving businesses, three well-adjusted (and at times, very opinionated and free-thinking) women as daughters, and the love of a man I have loved for thirty-four years (at the time of this book's release). And I didn't arrive at this place all on my own. I owe so much of it to the many qualified human beings who helped me land here. I spent so many hours in therapy.

LIKE. SO. MANY.

All of which helped me come to a very healthy understanding of me and the role I played in my intimate relationships.

And one of the most powerful things I learned during my own healing journey was whenever I was feeling "triggered" in a situation, like when somebody was doing something to me that was causing me to go into a survival reaction, was to stop and ask myself this one question: "What is the common denominator in this difficult time you're experiencing with _____ and _____ and _____?"

The answer I came up with was always the same.

The common denominator was me.

I discovered that I needed to own my shit in all the conflicts I was experiencing in my life. And when I began to take ownership and start to change how I was reacting to everyone and everything around me, let me tell you what happened: life got much more peaceful. Instantly more peaceful. And for a mouthpiece, shit disturber, run head first into conflict sort of woman like me, I have to confess to you, I had no idea that life didn't have to be so intense. Not everything needed to be debated. I didn't need to fight with every naysayer on the internet. I didn't need to get the last word. I didn't need to be right. And not every debate needed to be won.

Wow! Wow! Wow! Coming from a family where the person who yelled the loudest for the longest amount of time won, this revelation was HUGE. Like massive to my quality of life and to my relationships.

This began to roll downhill. Once I understood the power of owning my shit and being honest with my part in a conflict, I started to offer this wisdom to my daughters. Whenever my girls were having repetitive troubles in their relationships with friends, family, coworkers, or in their intimate relationships, I would ask them the same simple question: "What is the common denominator here? You. You are. Everywhere you go, there you are. Figure out who you are, what you need, what you can and cannot tolerate, and it will eliminate most if not all of the issues in your relationships."

Once I turned the tables around and asked myself the exact same question, I came to realize that my level of dissatisfaction with my marriage, with my career (or lack of one), and with my accomplishments had nothing to do with my husband and everything to do with me.

I was empty.

I was lost.

I was unhealed.

I was so dissatisfied with everything that had to do with me and what I had hoped, thought, and anticipated life to be like by the time I hit my midthirties that I honestly didn't know how or where to even begin to change any of it. Up until that point, I thought I had spent sixteen years building a life, and really all I had done was spend those years completing tasks, checking things off of a never-ending list of things to do. I'd run a ton of errands. I'd read copious amounts of books, children's books mostly. I'd cooked thousands of meals, packed hundreds of lunches, and clocked tens of hundreds of thousands of kilometers. I had done a lot, but none of it pertained solely to me or to my own mental well-being.

Because like you, I worked out (I even owned a gym at one point), I did my hair and my nails. I had girlfriends who I had girls' nights out with. I traveled alone. I even got massages! LOOK OUT!

Outwardly, I looked like I had it all together, and inwardly, I truly thought I did too. I mean, I didn't hate my busy, full life. Not at all. I was quite happy.

Until I wasn't.

I could bore you with all the details, give you the grocery list of reasons as to why I wasn't happy, but that would likely take up the entire book, and this is not meant to be a series unto itself. Suffice it to say that it hit me over the head like a hammer one day, and once it did, I could no longer pretend that I was okay. That my life was okay. That what had happened to me was okay.

I came to the painful realization that I never healed me.

And then it was like: "Oh, shit. So now what? What do I do now?"

I hit the wall, big time. I didn't want to do it anymore. Any of it. I wanted off the mommy hamster wheel. I wanted to take off my good wife hat. I wanted, no wait, let me rephrase this: I NEEDED to figure out who I was so I could figure out what I needed.

I needed to do the inner soul work so I could ensure that this one life, the life I've always said to my daughters is "both simultaneously too short and too long to spend it not living your passions" was one I would love living. Not one I would dread facing day in day out until I died. I didn't want to simply exist, I wanted to LIVE. I didn't want to *Groundhog Day* my life. I wanted to live life fully, wholly, and wide awake. I didn't want to be numbed by alcohol.

So, I did it. I started to do the work to uncover the mysteries of my own soul's desires. To unlock my own passions. To chart my own course of what a joyful, fulfilling life looked like for me. And all I can say is thank the fucking skies above that I got to do it in peace and quiet and privacy, because if I had to do it today, with social media, I don't know if I would have been able to do such a complete and authentic reboot on me if I was constantly looking outward to see how other people were healing, finding, and recreating themselves. There was a purity and an innocence as it were to my rediscovery of me because I got to do it by listening to my own heart, to my own intuition, with very few outside influences. In fact, in my adult rebranding, I lost an entire group of friends that I had truly come to love, count on, and thoroughly enjoyed. There were a lot of tears. Sad ones. Frustrated ones. Happy ones. It was a difficult but fruitful time.

As I shared with you earlier, I don't know why you picked up this book of mine. I have absolutely no idea where you are in your life journey. But if you're still reading this, then I hope you're ready to become really good friends. Because we're about to become super close. I'm going to share things about myself in these pages that I hope will inspire you to ask yourself some tough questions, to dig deep within yourself, to really examine where you're at in this life and if you're as happy as you could be. Whether you're doing a good enough job loving yourself. Because let's be honest here, it's not a BS statement, you know the one that "you can't expect somebody to love you, if you don't love yourself first." It's a fact. People will only love, respect, and honor you at the same level you love, respect, and honor yourself. You will

People will only love, respect, and honor you at the same level you love, respect, and honor yourself.

only ever get out of every single relationship you have in life whatever you put into you. People take your lead, so if you find that you're constantly being pushed aside, not taken seriously, not being authentically heard, then you have to ask yourself if you're even listening to you.

My guess is if you're still holding this book in your hands, you probably aren't doing any of those things very well at all. Or maybe you're still holding this book cuz you're my mom or one of my super close friends and you're just out here supporting me. If that's the case, then I just want to say thank you. However you got here to hang out with me, I'm glad you're here, and I want you to know if you feel like you don't even know how to begin putting yourself first and taking care of yourself . . . put your oxygen mask on first, am I right?! Have no fear, because now you have me. I've been in your shoes. And I've got you.

> Have no fear, because now you have me. I've been in your shoes. And I've got you.

I can totally help you get there. To that place of—as one of my new favorite badass brilliant authors Sonya Renee Taylor taught me in *The Body Is Not an Apology: The Power of Radical Self-Love*—prioritizing yourself in a way that isn't all encompassing or off balance so that your kids, your intimate partnership, and your friendships (basically all your outside relationships) suffer because you're suddenly at retreats every other week of your life. You're not going to become a professional narcissist, you're simply going to get in touch with you, your needs, your desires, and pour some love back into yourself so you get more out of your relationships and your actual life. To put it bluntly, all those people closest to you will get more of YOU out of you. And really isn't that what we all want out of our time here on Earth?

To love and to be loved, wholly, fully, and completely.

Let me help you get there. Because if this woman healed a traumatic childhood at the hands of an alcoholic, cheating father, and at boys and men treating me like a sexual object from the time I was nine until I found a good one to date at eighteen, and marry at twenty, then hell, you sure as shit can get it done too! I know you can because I did it, and I know you're going to do it too.

How this book works

This book wasn't written in a traditional way with chapters. I've written this book in phases. The first one is Your Past. In this section, you will look at the things that have happened to you before your today. We'll explore all the things that have built you and made you who you are. We will look at how these habits and patterns are blocking you and keeping you where you are right now.

I like to look at myself like a beautiful house, a temple. And this first part of my book is what I like to call the demolition stage. This is where we are going to strip away the old you, remove all the things about you that are completely run down, out of date, and no longer functioning. Demo happens to be my favorite part of every single renovation I've ever done. It's the most visually exciting because you see nothing but new possibility before you!

The second section, aptly called Your Present, is talking about your here and now, what is going on right now in your life. Where you're at, where you're stuck. While your past looked at and brought to the surface your old patterns and habits, in this section, we'll really dig into them, and together, we'll devise the plan to get you headed toward the new life you crave, long for, and deserve. This is where you'll lay a strong foundation and build the framing for your renovation.

The third and final section of my book takes you into the action phase, what I like to call the getting shit done phase. In Your Future, we'll make sure you have all your ducks in a row to continue following the new architectural drawings that we'll create together so you can build the exact perfect house (a.k.a. self) you want to spend the rest of your life living in!

As I mentioned at the very beginning of this book, I've created a *Without Losing Your Cool* journal, and I strongly recommend you purchase it to use in tandem with this book. It was made by me using the daily habits that this A-type personality found most helpful in reinforcing the positive thoughts, habits, and focus that I use to help me stay centered in gratitude and concentrated on keeping my eye on the prize of my own mental wellness, without all the positive toxicity.

Because let's be honest, since we're such good friends now, you're allowed to have shitty days. You're allowed to rest from doing hard work on yourself. You're fully free to be "off," to not want to nurture or to have rainbows shining out of your ass every single day of your life. It's okay to take a break from being your BEST SELF because nobody can be 100 percent awesome day in, day out.

It is IMPOSSIBLE.

I don't care how many affirmations or mantras you say in the mirror. I don't care how much chanting you do on your meditation pillow in your special, beautifully decorated meditation room overflowing with Buddhas, chimes, and incense.

I truly don't care how much of this you're surrounded with or if it got you off drugs, alcohol, or other things with these practices. That's all good and well, and there's power in ALL OF IT! I know there is because I implement a great many of these positive techniques in my daily life. I'm just saying that often even when you're doing all this shit, you still don't feel awesome. Bags of money still don't drop out of the sky into your living room. That perfect partner doesn't just show up in your life because you asked for them. It's okay to lose faith. It's okay to get exhausted from asking . . . waiting . . . trying. From believing the shit out of it. And when this happens, it is OKAY. In fact, it's more than okay if sometimes you just need a break. So, stop the work on yourself and just rest. Life is a marathon, after all. Pace yourself accordingly!

Sometimes you need to catch your breath and just LIVE your life as you are, rather than the notion that you're in constant need of a renovation or an upgrade. I mean you're not a fucking iPhone—you don't need a constant upgrade! You're a living, breathing human, and if you do the work and do it excellently, like building a home with a great set of architectural drawings and a solid foundation, all you're going to need at some point is regular maintenance. Not a full gut or teardown every damn day.

Think of yourself as a beautiful house that you've neglected for a decade or two, or maybe even more, so now you're in the full gut stage. It's a painful stage, and it might take longer and cost more than you wanted to spend, but in the end, because you'll have built it well, you'll only need to do maintenance for the next ten to fifteen years, then, and only then, you'll just need to do minor repairs and renovations. You'll never have to fully tear it down and rebuild it again. You get to just live in it—in peace, joy, and happiness.

Won't that be nice?!

Yes, yes, it will be absolutely heavenly!

So let's stop talking and let's start working! I'm going to help you learn to love yourself without losing your cool. Let's get to it!

YOUR PAST

Listen, if there was anyone who should have been voted most likely NOT to succeed, it is this girl right here. If you're new to our friendship, then might I suggest you grab yourself a glass, or a bottle, of wine, while I share a little bit of my past with you, and why the deck was stacked heavily NOT in my favor. And listen, don't worry about it, this book is in no way shape or form a victim book. I'm not going to drone on and on and tell you five ways from Sunday all the shitty things that were done to me as a young human being on this planet. That is so not the point of this book. Rather, it is about getting your shit together, not dwelling in it!

This book is about how to lay out your past in a journal, on a sheet of paper, in your phone, document the course thus far that you've been on, acknowledge it, thank it for making you, YOU, then moving the fuck on from it.

And not just like across the street or around the block from it. No, I'm talking about moving to an entirely new continent away from it. That's how far away we're getting into letting our shit go!

But I do need to share my past with you, so you can trust that I know what I'm talking about when I say that IF I can recover from my early life, to live a full, rich, blessed, and healthy life, then I have every faith and confidence that with me as your friend, sharing my knowledge and wisdom about what allowed me to live a life free of victimhood, you, too, will end up achieving the same. But YOU have to want it. YOU have to put in the work. YOU, my love, have to SHOW UP! I cannot show up for you. I cannot cheer you on enough to get you across the finish line. You need to fully commit here and now to doing the work.

Your Call to Action

Exercise: I want you to take five minutes to write on one of the blank pages at the back of your journal that accompanies this book and write out in a full-stream of consciousness, a letter of commitment to yourself, vowing to your spirit that you will put in the work during the course of this book, that you will show up for yourself 100 percent every single day while being on this journey with me. Take a few minutes to do this now.

If you've read any of my other books or my blogs, or listened to any of my interviews or my podcasts, you know that life didn't start off easy for me. Well, let me dial it back just a little bit. The beginning was pretty great; I mean, after I had two bouts of pneumonia before I was one. Actually, I guess if we go way back, it was pretty challenging right out of the gate, when I came out of said gate prematurely. As the story goes, I was small enough for my mother, who was eighteen and a mom to two by then (might I suggest that NOT teaching your kids about sex and how babies are made is a MASSIVE disservice and can and will more than likely turn into a teen pregnancy; but that is a story told in my two parenting books, which you should go buy if you haven't already) to be able to dress me in doll clothes. So, I guess looking ALL THE WAY BACK, the writing was on the wall that life was going to be a bit tougher for me than say the average unsuspecting, innocent child. And from that day forward of being born teeny tiny, and a bit too soon, it was a pretty wild ride.

Thank God for the way our brains work, that we don't intellectually remember much about life from in vitro and infancy. For me, memories are pretty sparse until around six or seven, when I can start to recall the way our apartment was decorated, the clothes I liked to wear, and the things I enjoyed doing to pass the time. The unfortunate part of our brains working this way is that the better parts of my childhood can't be recalled because I was too young, and it wasn't very long after when I was able to string a whole whack of memories together that they happened to not be very good ones. Causing me to wish that I couldn't recall them at all. I wish I could flip that on its ear, and recall the younger years, the time from two to nine, then only keep the beautiful memories of being nine to fifteen. Because I have to say there were so many good memories, like a shit ton, actually. But there are also so many heavy and confusing ones that literally cast a dark shadow over all the happy ones that it took me years to reconcile and release.

Maybe you're in that stage right now. The stage of only being able to recall and relive the ugly moments of your childhood, your teen years, your early adulthood, or fuck, your entire life until you picked up this book. Maybe you're still at that point in time of your life where you only see the cloud and not the sun no matter how much you meditate, how much you pray, how much you affirm and positive talk yourself out of the darkness. Perhaps like me you've spent thousands of dollars on therapy, coaching, medication even, and you still somehow can't shake off the weight of what was put upon you as a child, without your permission.

It's a pretty fucked-up thing being a kid, isn't it?

None of us asked to be born. We just showed up here, because maybe the two people who created you were in love. Maybe they're still in love, and that's pretty fucking awesome, odd, and unlikely, at least 50 percent unlikely, but totally amazing if they are. Maybe you were an accident, and the people who created you were like, "Well, we've got to do this thing now." And they tried and it didn't work out, and so you were raised by a single parent, who remarried, and you ended up with a massive family due to all the blending of all the kids who were made out of love. And unlike my father remarrying and having a whole other family, your new blended family was awesome and continues to be awesome. I don't know what your past is, which means that I have no idea what your story of how you came to be is, which is sort of not great for a friendship. You knowing so much about me and me knowing nothing about you . . . what I do know, very well, is my own story. I know that I'm a product of two very young hippies digging each other, but the young girl was not taught by her European immigrant parents how one makes a baby. So, at sixteen, my mother found herself pregnant. And when the nuns at the hospital tried to take the baby away from her to give him up for adoption, my mother knew, even at sixteen, that she wasn't going to be able to do that. She decided right then and there that this was HER CHILD, and she would be keeping him.

Pretty wild and crazy that she did that. And since she was estranged from her European family, as you can well imagine, she was literally ON HER OWN. I've said it once, and I'll say it a million more times before I die, I will never ever understand how my mother did that at sixteen. But she did. And then she did it again, having me at eighteen. LIKE WHAT?!

Yup. Mom of two at eighteen. No high school degree, no family support, just a teenage girl momming. Like a Christmas miracle, she somehow landed in a cafeteria that eventually resulted in a fantastic full-time office job with benefits and managing a whole team of people. Without a formal education.

My mother was a force.

My mother couldn't be broken. Defeated, yes, but broken, no.

My father, on the other hand, God bless him and all his horrific and tragic tales of woe. Not that my mother didn't have her own traumatic childhood, cuz she did, but she had a stronger character, whereas my father had an incredibly weak one. Now that I'm grown, lived a lot, known a lot of men, and watched my daughters and girlfriends date, it's hard to know if he had a flawed human character or if he was just an asshole man-boy. It's hard to say for sure. And I can't ask him any questions about all his past selfish choices, of drinking too much to the point of violence against us at home, or why he begged to come home every time my mom kicked him out if he was just going to cheat again. I can't ask him the whys of his life's choices because as fate would have it, he can't recall any of his life anymore. He has dementia and no longer remembers a damn thing.

Not sure if that's a blessing or a curse.

My mom says it's not surprising to her that this would be the way my dad gets to leave Earth, not even remembering all the pain and suffering he caused along the way. Yet we will forever remember it all too well. And so, those of us with our faculties in place will continue to have memories rise from the depths of our time with him that cause us to have to face, address, process, forgive, and release in order to continue on our journey in

It is so fucking magical to be living on the other side of trauma. this life. And here in lies the beginning of our work together, you and me. Together, we're going to see if my ability to move through my past successfully will assist you in doing the same. It is so fucking magical to be living on the other side of trauma. I lack the intellect or the vocabulary to express fully to you how insanely, profoundly beautiful it is to be here, where I am now. So, I wrote you this book, hoping that I can help you get to this point of bliss that I'm so thankful to be living in today. Let's walk the plank and jump into the deep unknown together.

I've got you!

Your Call to Action

Exercise: Using one of the blank pages in the back of your *WLYC* journal, create a list. I want you to write out your traumas. Something doesn't need to be dramatic to have been traumatic. It can be anything distressing or disturbing that you recall vividly as creating a huge mental shift in your life as you knew it. Keep this list until later; we'll be coming back to it.

Healing old wounds by letting go of trauma

Trauma can be something spontaneous like a car crash, a fire, or an unexpected death. It might be brought on through the experience of a robbery or destruction of your personal items. It could have been inflicted on you by bullying and name calling by your peers on the playground or in the locker room. Perhaps you were neglected by your parents, were left all alone for prolonged and unexplained periods of time, or had parents who withheld love and affection. Or, like me, it might have brought on accumulative traumas, such as being sexually, verbally, emotionally, and physically abused by a parent or relative.

Being hurt by being mistreated comes in all shapes, colors, and levels of intensity. This book is my story about mine and how I healed from it.

I've got to be completely transparent with all of you. I went back and forth, and back and forth, as to whether or not I should rehash my past in this book. Do I tell everybody about ALL the things that happened to me, that were done to me, that made me who I am today in order to get my point across to every single one of you reading this about how what happens to you isn't the be-all and end-all of who you become? How could I emphasize how much I'd conquered if nobody knows what it was

I was battling? I was like "how much is too much?" And I thought about all the people who will buy this book who have read my other books that already touched on my past. Is it redundant? Would it come across as though I am residing in "victimhood"? Will it upset those in my life who say it didn't happen? Who believe it was all made up?

I spent weeks at this point of my book, staring at the computer screen with my hands hovering over the keyboard.

Debating.

Worried.

Analyzing.

Concerned.

Conflicted.

Terrorized.

Guilt-ridden.

Anxiety-riddled about the potential negative impact or damage that the telling of my reality that made me who I am might have on those who didn't live it, and those who say they didn't do the things they did to me.

I was literally going back and forth internally debating on the importance, the relevance, and the accuracy of my history. Until I spoke to one of my best and wisest friends, who told me, "It is your story to tell. It happened to you, and whether the people who did it to you ever own it, you have the freedom to choose to share your story so that it might help another woman heal and work through her own unwanted sexual experiences. You have to write about your past authentically and let those other people worry about themselves."

It is not our job or our destiny to carry burdens, to be in pain.

So here I am, writing an authentic book about my past. Because I, like you, was not placed upon this Earth by chance. I was never brought here to suffer. It is not our job or our destiny to carry burdens, to be in pain. To carry the weight of other people's bad choices as if they were our own. As if the worst thing that could happen would be hurting the feelings or rocking the world of those who are guilty of committing the acts. Why is it ingrained in our psyche that we should suffer the act committed against us, then also protect those people above ourselves? That in and of itself is the definition of madness: honor the well-being of your perpetrator above the well-being of yourself?

But all too often that's exactly how it goes. Time and time again victims stay silent about the crimes committed against them, internalizing them, attempting to justify how those who tell you that what happened to you wasn't really that bad. "You're alive, aren't you?" Or "All kids get called names, it's part of being a kid." Or "You were only raped once, so many women have had to endure rape over and over and over again." As if you should compare your trauma to somebody else's trauma, because let's be frank here, there is always, without a shadow of a doubt, somebody who has suffered greater pain, loss, violence, poverty, and hardship than you. Always.

But trauma isn't a competition.

Your trauma can be that you had an inappropriate level of responsibility during your childhood in that you had to care for your adult parent, either due to an addiction or their illness.

Simply because millions of others may have suffered more than you doesn't mean that your trauma never happened. It doesn't mean that you're not still carrying your trauma around in the cells of your body. It certainly doesn't mean that whenever you hear a certain sound or when the entire world around you is dark that you're not immediately thrust back into the exact moment in time that it happened to you. The body is a tricky thing, and it has many cool little places to hold on to these sorts of pains long after you've done the healing. The forgiving. The "getting over it" of it all. And it can flip like a switch where you find yourself back in fight or flight mode. You know what that is, right? When your cells believe that you're likely going to die, so you get a rush of adrenaline and cortisol into your blood stream so you can successfully get yourself out of harm's way. And this, my friends, is no way to live. In fact, I had absolutely no idea that I was still holding onto the fear of being all alone in a house in spring 2021. It was the first time since I was eighteen that I found myself all alone in a house; because even when we were separated and Yannick had our girls for the weekend, I still had a big dog in my house. But it was that time in LA when Yannick took my four-legged protector with him when he had to move back to Toronto before me because of a directing gig that shit started to get weird. He had taken our youngest girl, her pup, and our boxer with him, and away they went on their travels. For two weeks leading up to his departure, I was weird. I was weepy. I was edgy. I was impatient. I just wasn't *me*. It was like I was mad at him although he had done nothing. I thought it might be because I was sure I was going to miss him. Normally, we have a rule where we try not to go more than two weeks without seeing one another, but because of COVID, this was going to be more like a month. So I thought I was being sucky and preemptively missing him.

And then it hit me.

On the very first night of being all alone in a house I barely knew, in the mountains of LA, I realized that what was going on with me was fear. I was afraid. It had been thirty-three years since I had been all alone in a house. By myself. With nobody else by my side. With no big dog beside me. I uncovered that what was driving my fear was the fact that every single bad thing that had ever happened in my life had taken place in my home. My haven. My safe space. Or what should have been a safe place for me to be. But it wasn't. And I know that I am not alone in feeling like that. I know that I'm not the only human being who is continuously doing the work to remind themselves that they're safe. That they're okay in their home. I'm sure that I'm also not the only woman who compulsively checks all her doors three times to make sure they are locked. I am confident that even though my trauma is behind me, the memories of it live on in these safety rituals.

You see, I didn't write this book because I'm completely over my fear and anxiety. I didn't write this book because I have kicked the ass of my fear and no longer suffer a day from it. No, I'm not done with it; I haven't conquered it. Not at all. I wrote this book because as somebody who lives with the reality of it, I was sick to death of reading books about how easy it is to "just let it go" or to chant or to meditate my way out of it. Toxic positivity had only gotten me so far. Therapy and life coach Leisse Wilcox got me into the end zone, but the thing with trauma is that it is ALWAYS WITH ME. Always. It forms which route I'll drive home in the dark. It dictates if I travel alone, and if I do, how far I will go.

But the super awesome thing about my journey of living with trauma is that I have incredibly and successfully learned how to not allow it to control me and my life. Or rob me of my dreams. Or leave me in a heap in the corner.

I decided a very long time ago that even though I could never take away what was done to me, I could very easily use it to my advantage. Because I know it's totally cliché, but baby, what doesn't kill you makes you stronger!

Can I get an A-FUCKING-MEN?!

Because we were never ever meant to spend this one beautiful, magical life void of joy, peace, or reconciliation. There is an answer for every single thing that comes our way. We may not see it in the moment; and we may find ourselves scratching our heads and asking the heavens above about ourselves or somebody we love, "Why does bad stuff happen to good people?"

I don't have the answer to that, per se, but in a blanket response, something that I've come to believe over my years and years of facing my trauma is that it is all here to teach us.

To the women reading this who have lost children to tragedy, either through violence or illness, I am not saying in any way shape or form that I understand your pain, your grief, your agony. I see you . . . my heart aches for you, and like you, I still ask that question, "Why?" I am not being flippant to your anguish and your suffering, which is completely different to mine. Or that of a woman who lives in poverty, without enough money to feed herself or her children properly. I'm not diminishing trauma or comparing one with being easier to overcome than another. I'm not here to categorize or rate traumas. Vanessa Bryant comes to mind to show that you can have it ALL, and I mean ALL, then one regular Sunday morning you lose both the love of your life and a child in one unexpected fell swoop. Gone. Never to be held by you again.

That's traumatic.

And it is merciless and brutal.

My trauma was brutal too.

Yours was also.

All trauma is a complete blow to the parasympathetic nervous system because it comes out of left field. It's unexpected. Sudden. An instant shift to your "normal," which makes it so difficult to release. It gets in DEEP to your cellular memory.

Are you familiar with the parasympathetic and sympathetic systems that our bodies operate off of? They are the systems responsible for our bodies reacting and relaxing.

The sympathetic nervous system is responsible for how our body responds during times of stress or emergency and floods our body with cortisol when we're under distress. It decides if we stay (fight) or if we run like hell (flight) when we sense any type of danger. It's our trauma response system, which comprises the six Fs (freeze, flight, fright, flag, fawn, and faint). I don't know about you, but I for sure have experienced all of these different physical reactions while in the thick of trauma.

The parasympathetic nervous system is responsible for conserving the body's energy by slowing the heart rate and boosting the activity of glands and intestines while the body is resting. It's the opposite of the sympathetic nervous system. All good, right?

According to some medical journals, the parasympathetic nervous system isn't as important to staying alive as the sympathetic one; and herein lies the problem for so many of us who think that living in the thick of trauma and under stress is more normal than living in a relaxed, calm state. Things that make me go "hmmm," indeed. Shouldn't we be striving to engage our parasympathetic nervous system more often? Especially since we know spikes in cortisol lead to so much illness and stubborn weight gain, which are only a couple of the negative side effects of constantly living in fight or flight.

Look, I'm not shitting you when I tell you that it's paramount to the quality of the rest of your life that you literally need to heal your past right away—like yesterday. Unhealed, unresolved trauma, whether it be sexual, physical, or verbal abuse, is insidious, and not only does it steal your todays, it has the ability to ruin all of your tomorrows too. Here's some information about just how toxic unhealed trauma can be:

- People with unresolved trauma are much more likely to develop diseases such as heart disease, cancer, liver disease, and diabetes.

- When someone goes through a traumatic event, the negative emotions around that event get trapped in their body. It's not just your mind that remembers the pain, your body remembers it too. That's why we often feel sad or scared or sick when we remember a painful event. Our body holds on to that negative energy. Don't know where you're at with your trauma, but I can attest to the physical and psychological distress as being 1,000 percent a thing!

- Angry, hurt, sad, or scared people live in angry, hurt, sad, or scared bodies. And until they address those underlying issues, their body will hold on to that negative energy.

- To change and to heal, you must be in tune with your body and your emotions. You can't focus on one while ignoring the other.

- Quantum Physics tells us that everything has its own frequency, its own energy. Everything. And every cell contains information (memories) about it. And when those memories contained in our bodies are negative, the overall effect is negative.

- You might try and block the trauma from your memory, but your cells can't ignore it. They'll hang on to that trauma in its raw form, regardless of whether you're ready to deal with it. Maybe you grew up with a parent who yelled a lot, and when you were little, you held your breath and tensed up. You might be unaware that you still automatically stiffen up and freeze whenever you hear shouting. That's because your body still remembers your reaction to the trauma. It's become an automatic reflex.

- If you experience three or more traumatic experiences in your life, you're at an elevated risk for developing physical or mental problems. This is further proof that I really had no shot at heading into adulthood as a well-adjusted woman.

- Trauma also has a direct result on how memories are stored. Often toxic memories end up as disjointed images or sensations. Fragmented memories are an example of dissociation, which can prevent the healing process and increase the risk of serious symptoms often associated with post-traumatic stress disorder (PTSD).

There is so much more information out there about how trauma affects the body and your mental fortitude—or lack of it. I mean, fuck, three or more adverse childhood experiences or traumas? Just having my father as a father took me over this marker. It's no wonder I've had days where I was breaking down, confused, angry, and bitter . . . seemingly for no good reason. Some days, I felt like I wanted to die.

You may be reading this and scratching your head thinking:

"But you have your health?" Yes, I do, and some days I still wanted to die.

"But you have a long-lasting love affair with a partner who loves you?" Yes, I do, and some days I still wanted to die.

"But you have three healthy, loving, beautiful daughters who love you?" Yes, I do, and some days I still wanted to die.

"But you are beautiful, you have two successful companies, you are moderately famous?" I know. I know. But some days I still thought about dying as a form of escaping the hell I sometimes had to deal with inside my head.

Unprovoked.

Some days I lie quietly in my bed, tears streaming down my face, for no good reason, and all I can think is: "Wouldn't my family be better off if I just wasn't here anymore?"

"Would I really miss all that much if I just stopped living?"

"Would anybody even miss me?"

... healing the shit that happened to you is not the same thing as never having experienced the shit.

This is trauma. This is mental illness. This is a wounded psyche. This might be you too.

I've learned over the many, many years of inner work that healing the shit that happened to you is not the same thing as never having experienced the shit.

Read that again!

Just because you put in the work, just because you've faced the demons head on and looked them in the eyes and reclaimed your life, your fortitude doesn't mean that the thing that sometimes, like me, might make you think, even all these years later, like you may want to die is gone forever. What it does mean is that you now have the tools to pull yourself up out of that bed or off the floor and remind yourself that you're a child of God and worthy of a full, rich, complicated, and beautiful life.

Your Call to Action

Exercise: While I have you in the thick of your own past trauma experiences from reading about mine, take a few minutes to write down in your journal what your trauma was that blocked you from seeing your worth, your value, your importance in this world. And write about whether or not it got so bad, like mine has, that you thought life was done with you.

The fact that I survived almost daily sexual trauma from age nine to fifteen seems like a miracle. Especially when you add in the father neglect, exploitation, and abandonment. It's always a shock to me that I "turned out" as well as I have. But it wasn't easy. It took years of wading through the guck to get to the good stuff in life. I believe one of the things that brought me my greatest healing was becoming the mother of three women. Even though as a young woman I believed that I would never—should never—be a mother because I wasn't sure I would be able to love and protect them, God, the Divine, the Universe knew better. It knew that by having these children, it would heal so much in me. With my ability to protect the three of them from the same cycles of sexual abuse that I suffered by marrying a human being who was nothing at all like my father so they would know male love, kindness, and affection in a healthy way propelled the injured little girl in me into a much more stable and confident emotional state. Now, that's not to say that I wasn't what some might view as over protective of them. Hell, they might even say so themselves, but at least I got them through their lives without them having to wear trauma their entire lives. This is why I'm so focused on doing enough, spreading my message, writing my books, and trying to make the world a better place by the people I'm sending out into it. I mean, now that you know all this about my past, is it really any surprise that I wrote books about how to raise decent humans considering how much I had suffered at the hands of so many who had not been raised well? I think not.

Some of you might have a history of trauma, like me, who want to break that cycle. Some of you might be a parent, like me, who want to find a way to stop the intergenerational trauma. Some of you reading this might even have children who are nine, the same age I was when the abuse started.

One of the ways that I was able to protect my girls was to guard my baby bears like my life—and theirs—depended on it. This is why I harp on it SO MUCH in my parenting books that we parents need to be ALERT, AWARE, and PROTECTIVE of our children. I say it *ad nauseam*, "It takes two minutes for your kid's life to be changed forever." It did for me. Apart from my father coming home in drunken, sometimes violent stupors, until the sexual trauma started, I have extremely fond and deeply happy memories of my childhood.

Like one of my best memories was when I got to share a bedroom and a bed with my mom. My father was out of the house, again, for being a runaround. So my mother, to make ends meet, because my father never paid child support when he wasn't living with us, had a coworker move into our apartment and rent my room. I had no idea that this was a "bad thing" to have to do. I mean, I'm confident my mother was having zero fun sharing a bed with her young daughter, but it was a happy time for me. I felt blessed that I was the only girl in the family because I got to be my mom's roommate. Now that I look back on it as a mother of three women myself, I realize that it really shouldn't have been what one would call a "happy memory," yet it was. I dare say that what we don't know can't hurt us is powerfully true. It certainly was in my case of being a young kid who was having the best time of her life being her mom's roommate. I don't recall missing my father at all. But looking back now, I can see how incredibly painful, difficult, and upsetting it must have been for my mother. Although you could never tell. She seemed happy to me. It's probably the same way I seemed happy to my girls, and the way you right now might seem happy to your inner circle.

But such was the case for most of my childhood, having no idea how bad, how wrong things were around me. Believing the shit that I was living was actually "normal." Listen, I'm not over here saying I had the worst life ever, I'm living life with my eyes WIDE OPEN. I know there are some of you who have withstood some absolutely unspeakable horrors. I've had some women share their abuse with me, which has caused me to catch my breath and weep with them as they share devastatingly heartbreaking truths about what they endured. I see you. I hear you. And if I've said it once, I'll likely say it a million times: this book is not a competition of who was abused more or to have people write in to tell me that my abuse was nothing compared to theirs. I'm not here to compete with you and your trauma, at all. I'm here as a friend, as somebody who wants to support you in the knowing that as awful as it was, it doesn't have to remain awful anymore. There is healing. There is relief. There is releasing. And there is bliss out there for you to claim. I want to go on the journey with you where you get to the point where you not only step into your power, but you claim it and you spread it around, empowering other women in your circle, or damn, even outside of your circle to own it. Spread your strength.

I was only nine when I learned things about being female that I would have much preferred to learn when I was older and at my leisure.

Did it freak me out?

Yes. Fuck, yes! It did.

Did I do anything about it?

Fuck, no.

Cuz, I mean, aren't all boys this way? Aren't all kids like this, innocently sexually curious?

Don't all older brothers do nothing when their friends tell them that they're going to spy on their younger sister naked?

I mean, I didn't know. How could I? I was so young.

I really thought that it was kids being kids, boys being boys. Now I know that being raised with this bullshit guise has created so many fucked-up men who have sexually assaulted women. There was definitely some thinking back then that boys were allowed to do this sort of thing. There was even some victim blaming going on. My personal favorite gaslighting phrase to excuse my childhood sexual abuse is: "Well, you asked for it. Wearing bikinis at the public pool around them, and playing spin the bottle with all those kids who were four to six years older than you. This *is* YOUR fault."

NO! It's not. I know now that this is total and absolute bullshit. There is a massive difference between consenting to participate in a game of spin the bottle and to boys hiding in your closet waiting to see you naked, then touching you inappropriately WITHOUT YOUR CONSENT.

According to The National Children's Advocacy Center (NCAC), most kids are sexually curious with others starting as young as age five. But there's a massive difference between curiosity and abuse.

But as a young female, when you've engaged in not exactly "age appropriate games" with all older kids, how do you then go to your parent to tell them that the older kids have now decided to take the "game" too far?

You don't.

So, boundaries are never created. And before you know it, you end up being raped at eleven.

And guess what you do about that? You take ownership of it. You blame yourself. Because since sex has been brought to the table by older kids, but I never told anybody about it—and in fact, I'd begun to engage with it—this must all be my fault. I thought, "Well, I do have breasts already, and I wear tight jeans, so I was totally asking for it."

It's a complete mindfuck!

I don't know what you're battling, what trauma you're working at healing from, but I would venture a guess that there is some part of you that feels responsible. Where you believe that you own some of the reason *why* life came at you the way that it did. That you essentially got what you deserved.

You say nothing because you secretly believe it's your fault.

So, you walk through life like this for years. And when you have this shame, it's almost like other pedophiles, other abusers, can smell it on you. Like they know you've been broken, and they know that you think it's your fault. So, they can also abuse you, because well, you're never going to tell anybody . . . because you started asking for it SO MANY YEARS AGO.

And on and on and on goes the cycle of allowing men to abuse you.

Until one day, you wake up and realize that as a female you can want to be curious about sex without somebody then groping/fondling/touching you without your consent.

When you learn that you can kiss someone without it meaning that they can have sex with you without your consent.

One day, when you grow up, if you're lucky enough to have a strong group of girlfriends, you can ask them if the trauma that was so common place in your life ever happened to them. And what you might learn is that yes, a friend of yours does have a similar life story. Or like me, you will come to learn that not a single other friend had any stories like what had happened to you. Not one. And this knowledge would then become your hint to tell somebody who could A) stop it or B) help you get help to heal from it.

I mean, let's be honest, most women suffer some sort of sexual abuse in their lifetimes at the hands of a lover. Sometimes it's from a friend who wants to be a lover and they try to take it on their own accord. For victims of sexual abuse, it often doesn't happen over so many years and not at the hands of so many different people.

But fuck! So many of my girlfriends have stories. Most have at least one story of a man taking more than he was offered sexually. And the fact that I'm sitting here writing this book without a shadow of doubt that so many women have at least one horror story pertaining to unwanted sexual advances from a man. This fact was a massive reason why I wrote my parenting books—because parents of sons must do better. They must raise men who don't believe that sexual interaction with women is like living out their own porno. Males need to be taught the reality of consent. That without consent there is no sex. Parents need to teach their sons about what is and what is not an appropriate game to play with people of the opposite sex. What age kissing and touching should start happening. We need to talk to our boys as in-depth about sex as we do our girls. We're always telling our girls how NOT to get pregnant, how NOT to get raped, but let's start teaching our sons how NOT to be that guy who feels entitled to sexualize a female simply because he wants to.

Can I get an AMEN?!

It's not somebody else's daughter's responsibility to raise your son into a good man. Parents of sons must teach their boys to be respectful of women, all women. It is imperative that men treat women as equals, as worthy, especially when it comes to sexual desire. This is nonnegotiable.

Alright, so now that we've handled that, we're at the part of the first section where I want you to do some self-digging. I've shared my birth to fifteen with you in the hopes of helping you feel comfortable, safe, and not alone in your trauma. I told you that I've got you, and I totally do.

Your Call to Action

Exercise: Now is the time when you're going to crack open your journal and take some time to write out your past.

Your history.

Many of you won't have had any physical trauma, and that's a good thing. But what you might have is emotional or psychological trauma. Perhaps you were neglected by one or both of your parents. And this doesn't need to look like your parents were alcoholics or abused drugs; it could simply be that they were super busy with their careers or social lives. Maybe you were more like an accoutrement to their meals and not the entrée. Maybe you were raised by nannies; or worse, you raised yourself, waking yourself up for school, making your own breakfast, your own lunch, taking yourself back and forth to school, having no support with school work, having nobody leading you, leading yourself. Not ideal. It isn't exactly "abuse" when parents feel like they're doing you a solid by having you make your own way through this wild ride called life. But their hands-off parenting style might have left you developing the subconscious "belief" that you're not important. That your needs don't matter. That the only person you can and should rely on is yourself. So you build these imaginary walls to live inside of because what's the point of letting anybody in—nobody would actually want to be there with you if your own parents didn't want to be. This is trauma. This is pain. And that gets trapped inside your cells and needs to be addressed, dealt with, and healed.

Another way you may have experienced trauma is through emotional or verbal abuse:

"You're always so loud."

"Nobody cares what you think."

"Thank God you're cute because you're not very smart."

"Oh God, why are you so heavy? Momma can barely lift you."

"Don't eat that."

"When I was your age . . ."

"If you only had my work ethic."

On and on and on it might have gone during your formative years. The comments seemed innocent because they weren't loud, aggressive, or violent. Verbal degradation can be something that seemed like "small talk" or "nothing serious," but day in, day out, it strips away any likelihood that you'll have any self-esteem. This one is so insidious because it doesn't need to be loud. The person committing this sort of abuse against you doesn't need to be obvious or blatant: "Oh, here let me do this for you, you're not any good at it" or "Should you be eating that?" These small little digs just need to be consistent.

As children, we're often given incorrect information about ourselves and the world at large, but because it comes from the "big people" in our lives, it must be true. It must be accurate. It must be gospel. And so it becomes the lens that we observe life through.

This information is inaccurate because it's colored with and by the adult's life and experiences around you. But you're little, so how or why would you know that? You wouldn't, so it just becomes the absolute truth from which you operate. We ride hard for that information and the adults who parlayed it down to us. The negative comments might have to do with our looks, our intelligence, or our ability: "Lisa is so pretty, but you know, she isn't very smart; that's her brother's department" or "Taylor isn't very strong or coordinated; they're more of a watch from the sidelines sort of kid."

Both of these comments might feel innocent enough, but it ends up creating a belief pattern in the brain that "I'm not smart, so I should focus on my looks," which might result in an obsession over appearance and body size and perhaps an impossible standard to live up to. I know, I tried for thirty-five years of my life to hold on to how I looked with a clenched fist, because I was 100 percent confident that I wouldn't be able to hold on to the love of my husband if I wasn't "beautiful." I spent tens of thousands of dollars on plastic surgery: liposuction at twenty-six; tummy tuck and breast implants after hitting 200 lb. after the birth of my third daughter at twenty-eight; removal of implants a few short years later; breast lift and reduction, to name just a few. My husband acted with *Playboy* Playmates on one of his series. My dad only paid attention to me for my looks, even to the point of parading me around people who were "above him" in life to prove his own worth. My first love only cared for me when I was thin enough for his liking. My dance teacher only let me dance in front as a lead when I was finally skinny like her. I was only ever rewarded with love or success based on how I looked, and so began the life cycle of hating myself in order to have others love me.

And what of the child who grows up being told they aren't big enough, strong enough? They might become a bully on the playground just to prove to everybody how tough and badass they are. Or they might never try something physically challenging, even if it sparks passion, because there's an internal loop playing inside their head: "Oh, I'll never make the team because I'm just not good enough."

We learn at a very young age to subconsciously self-sabotage because we don't want to contradict what we were told about ourselves as children by the people in our lives who loved us.

So how can you correct this and eliminate it from your self-consciousness? Especially if it's a pattern you may have been actively reinforcing, like me, for decades. How can you stop the disconnect of what you believe in your soul about who you *actually* are compared with who you've been *told* you are?

You must be willing to go against these inaccuracies that were put into you by others.

But how?

How do we even begin to undo the layers of muck? Trauma? Pain?

The great news is that you already have all you need right inside of you. It is called your inner authority. It is the boss of you, and all that you believe, think, and focus on. It really is quite simple, and it begins with reverse engineering the old patterns of belief, starting with "I am." If you were told you were stupid, fat, and clumsy, all you need to do is sit with those beliefs and write out and say the opposite out loud, louder than the people who dumped their shit and limiting beliefs onto you in the first place.

I am SMART. I am HEALTHY. I am STRONG. I am WORTHY.

Only YOU know what negative beliefs are ingrained in you, so only you know what positive truth you need to replace them with. Together, we are going to create a new main character in the TV show that is your life. It sounds simple, I know. And airy-fairy. It seems impractical that all of a sudden you'll just start standing in the mirror saying beautiful things to yourself, and voilà, you will be healed. All the years of verbal abuse will be washed away, and you'll be made whole and new again.

Not so fast. It's not just about saying words in the mirror—it's about actually fucking believing them! And you're likely a bit of an onion, meaning that there isn't just one thing holding you back in life. Like me, you might have many layers of abuse that you need to peel away and heal; so, we're going to be thorough and thoughtful about all of this.

We're not going to rush this process.

Hell, you don't even have to do it right this minute if you're not ready to.

This book is about supporting you in releasing your hurt, those terrorized pieces of you that have played a contributing factor in you not living your one life to its fullest.

So often we think our busyness is just that, us being busy. What I came to learn was that I kept myself extremely busy so I didn't have to think about the things that were still so deeply painful inside of me. I was busy distracting myself from getting to the bottom of the trauma, because it was already so difficult to live through the first time, wouldn't it just be so much better and way cooler to, you know, just have it magically melt away. Just disappear as if none of it ever happened?

I tried that for a really long time, and it was destroying me. It was destroying my marriage to an actual decent, kind, sensitive, and loving man, and it was causing me to exist in a self-sabotaging bubble.

Until I cleared it.

Our work in this book might not clear you all the way out. I read thousands of books before I got to THE book and the coach (Leisse Wilcox) who would ACTUALLY clear me.

She helped me bring my healing work into the end zone.

So, let me help you bring to light the shit that's holding you back, so you can start to do the work to get it gone. I got healed, and now it's your turn. It's all about paying it forward. Am I right?

Your Call to Action

Exercise: Open your *WLYC* journal, reflect on these questions, and write down your answers.

- What are your traumas?
- Who committed them against you?
- Did you tell somebody who could hold the other person accountable?
- Did you take any action to help you feel safe?
- Does this past trauma hold you back from living a rich, healthy, full life?

Mark the page with your responses; we're going to dig into them a little bit later.

Getting real about habits
and patterns that no longer
serve you

Alright. So, we've shared our pasts with one another. For most of us, it's not rocket science to uncover the patterns that have formed in us over the course of your time here on Earth. I mean, even dogs learn fairly quickly how to get what they want out of us—they don't call them puppy dog eyes for no reason!

I kid, I kid.

This is serious business. Loving yourself completely and prioritizing yourself is absolutely of paramount importance; yet so many of us do it haphazardly, putting it off until a better time. Now is that better time. Today is the day that you stop allowing yourself to hide behind negative patterns, habits, and behaviors that not only no longer serve you, but if we're being completely blunt with one another, have never served you. Not even one day in your life. Yet you use them and hang on to them like a badge of honor to remind yourself and everybody around you that you are a victim. That you have been victimized in your lifetime.

Well, I have a couple of questions for you:

1. How many people have you hurt through your self-sabotaging habits?

2. How many people are being held back from achieving what they've dreamed of in life by your negative patterns?

The answer to both these questions should be obvious to you. It's obvious to me—because I've done this too. And the bottom line is that the only person your behavior really hurts, holds back, and damages is you. Just you. The other people carry on their merry way through life, forgetting that they ever did anything to cause you pain or develop self-sabotaging patterns and habits.

So, my next question to you is this: If they're not reeling from the pain their actions have caused and they have moved on, why haven't you? What are you waiting for? How much longer will you live your life in the bottom of a bottle or hopped up on pills because it's better to be numb than to face your past? How long will you continue to eat yourself into illness? Or starve to punish yourself for not being "good enough" in the eyes of the adult who dumped their shit onto you? How many more nights do you want to spend being hyper-sexual, giving the most precious part of yourself away to people who don't deserve to know you in that way, because you've come to believe that you have no value, that you're not precious, that you're only a sexual object? How long are you going to continue to be angry, jealous, bitter, and envious of other people who are "living your life?" How much more time are you willing to invest in the obsession of scrolling through the highlight reels of other people's lives, while never ever putting those hours back into yourself to create your own life of highlights? How many more days do you want to spend gossiping, bitching, moaning, and complaining about your fate? How much longer do you want to keep pretending that you don't deserve to live a whole, happy, blessed, and healthy life?

Aren't you exhausted from trying to fit your giant, glorious, beautiful, perfect spirit into the box that others built for you?

Aren't you ready to show those who tried to dim your light that you will not be made small?

Aren't you ready to shine?

Be the lead character you want to be in your own life.

There's only one life, baby. It's all we've got—let's make it epic! Cuz I'm here to tell you, life is way more rewarding when you live it full-out, when you reclaim ownership over it, when you no longer make excuses about WHEN you're going to get better, do better, be better.

You have today; that's all you have.

It is our arrogance that allows us to procrastinate through life. It is our ego that lulls us into a false sense of comfort of believing that "You don't need to address _____ with _____ today. You can do that tomorrow. When you feel up to it. When you feel *ready* to do it."

The "when I am ready" tact to changing your unhappy circumstances is my absolute FAVORITE LINE OF BULLSHIT any of us tell ourselves.

Bitch, you are never ever going to be READY to get into the deepest corners of yourself, to lay yourself bare, exposed, so you can do the real work of healing. It's like saying, "I'm ready to start a family."

No. You. Are. Not. You might *think* you're ready. You might even *want* to start that family. But ready? Are you really? I'd say most of us were not. I sure as hell was not at nineteen, let me tell you that much for free. And some days, some LONG ASS DAYS of being a mom, I look at myself in the mirror with my hair in a topknot for the fifth day in a row and a face that needs washing, not because of any makeup that I'd put on it but from just living, and I think "damn, I was not ready for today."

And this is the beautiful, magical messy thing about life—we never know what it's going to throw at us. And we won't ever really be "ready," but we can be prepared, and we should start getting prepared today. Now. No more putting off until tomorrow what you can do today.

Why?

Well, what if another pandemic comes along and shuts down our entire existence again? What if the one we're still in ain't quite done with us yet? Then what? Then you'll have put off working on yourself, letting your shit go on (that not only no longer serves you, but in fact, never served you, not even once, not even for a hot minute) for another two years?

And what about the fragility of life?

What about the "no guarantee for tomorrow" reality that is life?

Why are we humans so convinced that we will have a life expectancy that lasts until 82.8 years (2021 average in Canada)? Because we're cocky, that's why. Even those of us who are timid and tend to live our lives a little bit more like the world is always ending still believe: "I've got time to have a better life, later."

In fact, as I sit at my keyboard today continuing with the writing of this very topic, I'm numb and operating on little sleep because one of the most beautiful human beings I know and am blessed to call a close friend let me know late last night that she has lung cancer. And cancer along her spine, her femur, her bones. She doesn't smoke. She just turned fifty. She has two daughters, one still in high school, the other in her first year of university. Years ago, she got up the nerve to leave her loveless marriage, even though her mother didn't want her to because her mother loved him that much. It took her years to win that battle within herself, due to the fear of upsetting her girls; every woman in a loveless marriage with kids suffers and struggles with this exact same fear that turns into guilt before the trigger of leaving is even pulled. And now, she's with her dream man, just bought her dream home, and this happens. Cancer. Everywhere.

It's unjust.

It's sudden.

It's out of the blue.

It's a living, breathing, in the moment example of the harsh, brutal reality that none of us have any idea what our future holds.

What is happening to my beautiful friend is what Esther Perel, the brilliant psychotherapist, wrote about. Two of her books that I believe any human being alive and breathing should read, whether in an intimate relationship or not: *Mating in Captivity* and *The State of Affairs*. What she speaks about in these books and what she teaches us about the way we operate in our lives and in our relationships with others is so powerful, so poignant that you can only learn and grow by reading her. What is happening to my amazing friend is what Esther would call a "life accelerator." Her health crisis is revealing to her just how short life is, and that it can come to a screeching halt at any second. The fucking incredibly fortunate thing for my dear friend is she's not a sit on her hands sort of woman; she is living her life out loud every single day. Thankfully. Luckily.

Are you?

Seriously. Honestly. Truthfully. Are you?

We don't have any guarantees. Not a single one. We have right now. This moment. This day. That's all we know for sure.

Every single minute of every single day that you spend playing Russian roulette with your life, waking up and choosing to spend one more second, minute, hour sitting in your shit, clinging to your useless stories that cripple you is time that you can never reclaim. If you got the same sort of news that my girlfriend just got, would you be able to say that you faced your demons, your fears, and went after the life you truly wanted in order to be whole? To be healed? To have joy?

I don't have any letters after my name, but what I do have is a laundry list of passions I pursued, dreams I went after, desires I satisfied, and ones that I continue to fulfill. I kicked the stories that were inputted into me by others to the curb; I didn't cave to them. I didn't let them run me or ruin me. I simply woke up every single day and decided the best revenge against people who tried to break me was to live a full, rich, larger-than-life life. Even on the days when I entertained the notion that death might be better than trying to heal me, I still refused to take shortcuts, or let dreams die on the vine. I took back my power. Those who abused me had already taken so much, a childhood marred by negative adult experiences, years of me being so angry at myself for bringing all this on.

I acknowledged it.

I faced it.

I wrestled with it.

I cleared it.

I let it go and I reclaimed my life. And in fairness to those of you reading this right now, it wasn't in one fell swoop. I healed parts and pieces along the way. Every layer revealing another area that needed love and kindness until I got to where I am today.

Fully in love with the body God gave me. Grateful for the way she has housed my strong spirit, my brilliant mind, and my generous heart. For carrying to full term, and delivering three healthy daughters. Forgiving myself for abusing her by denying her food when I thought I'd be more loved if I was skinnier, and drinking alcohol daily because it made not facing my past easier and life "more fun."

And writing this book for you. You. Who might be on the brink of throwing in the towel for good. You. Who might have just now suffered something traumatic. You. Who might have been made to believe your entire life you had no value.

The beautiful thing about being on this side of having done the work is that if like my beautiful and remarkable friend, I were to get such grim and devastating medical news, I could be like her, confident in the knowing that I didn't hold back. I didn't rip myself off with putting off building a life that I wanted to live. Would I be terrified? Yes. Absolutely. But like her, I would be at peace with that part of my situation. And the crushing thing to try and reconcile for me would be thinking about my girls and all the people I love and wanting more time. Which is precisely why in my darkest, bleakest, lowest moments of being almost tricked in to contemplating death, I didn't give in. I woke up to the knowing that I had way more life I wanted to live. I hope that if like me you have battled with the thought of suicide, you were guided back from the brink of it because of your love for life, with all her difficulties, upset, cruel, and unjust plot twists, you still found value in being alive. Hopefully your circle, your village, no matter how small it was or is, gave you reason to keep going. I hope you had the people, your people, who love you, who have always told you the truth in love beside you during your darkest times, to help pull you out of your emotional abyss. A village that holds you accountable, who loves you as you are, warts and all, who help you reside outside your trauma and in the beauty, the real beauty, of life.

Your pep squad. We all need one of these.

Your Call to Action

Exercise: In your *WLYC* journal, write about your pep squad. Name them. Identify their role in your life. Write them a note of gratitude. Share it with them, or don't, but make your gratitude specific when you write about it.

Time is our most precious
commodity

And I think we can all agree that when our end comes, no matter what age we will be when that happens, we will likely all say and feel the exact same way: "I just want more time."

You see, the human species has managed to replicate a lot of things. We've learned how to algorithm the shit out of life. We even have robots that can do pretty much everything you and I can do, but no technology can reclaim time that is lost. Once time is gone, it is gone forever.

Don't let that be your fate. While you still have air in your lungs, legs that can carry you, and a mind that has dreams, now is the time to take action to move out of the patterns and habits that no longer serve you. Look in the mirror and ask yourself this: "What in the hot fresh hell are you waiting for?"

Today might be your last day. I'm not being morbid, I'm just pointing out, if life has taught us anything since late 2019 is that it really could be. SO WAKE UP!

If you are waiting for a sign that now is the time to build the life you've always dreamed of, let me help: I am your sign. NOW IS THE TIME!

Let what I just shared about my incredibly beautiful friend be your sign.

And if all of this so far in the first 100 pages of my book is not enough to shake you loose, get you actively participating in the healing of your old habits and patterns that no longer serve you, then please do yourself a favor and order every single book that Gary John Bishop has ever written and have them delivered to your door:

Unfu*k Yourself

Do The Work

Stop Doing That Sh*t

Wise as Fu*k

> ... it really is within us to be able to get through and over our trauma.

His no-nonsense, non-flowery, you literally have all the power within yourself to heal your shit attitude is life changing. It takes living life without excuses to another level. Like going to the Super Bowl of your healing level. Ultimately, let's call a spade a spade, it really is within us to be able to get through and over our trauma. We have what it takes—we just need to do it. We truly need to decide to heal it. Today is the day to start living your whole life. I've done it. So many others have done it, and I have every confidence in you that you're going to do it too. Because remember, the amazing positive thing about being "fucked up" is that you're not alone.

I've got you!

Your Call to Action

Exercise: In your *WLYC* journal, create a list of:

- Habits you have that you know are keeping you from changing and creating the life you desire.
- Patterns of thought that you have developed that keep you stagnant in your life.
- Negative self-talk that plays on a loop and lives rent free in your head.

Releasing attachment to your old stories

So, we've decided that the behaviors, patterns, and habits that we've been clinging to are no longer our friends. And in fact, with some deep exploration, including reading this book, Gary John Bishop's and Esther Perel's books, and with coming face-to-face with the reality of just how fragile life is, we're now going to move on to the part where we release our love affair with our old stories. Some of them are probably sick and twisted, while simultaneously being somehow strangely comforting, like that suckie blanket you kept until you were twelve that smelled like death no matter how often it was washed. It simply had too many years of sleeping breath breathed into the fibers of it to smell like anything else. That's like our attachment to our old damaging stories: they stink to high heaven, to the point of potentially being toxic, yet we hold them fast.

Some of you reading this might be wondering what old stories I'm talking about. What I mean by stories is the person (people) who live inside your head, who tell you that you're not smart enough, good enough, pretty enough, thin enough, or rich enough to count. To matter. To weigh in on the world around you. That you are unworthy of joy, love, success, peace, health, or even of being alive. The narrative that plays inside our heads can be completely debilitating to the point where we are in a constant state of paralysis. Your paralysis might be that you have difficulty making decisions. Maybe you're indecisive to the point where you cannot make a move unless you consult with at least half a dozen people in your life. And if you don't get a clear, definitive answer from your group, you won't make any decision at all. Or even if you do get a complete answer, you're so riddled with insecurity that you still won't move. So you stand stuck exactly where you are, where you were last year, last decade, or maybe where you've been stuck your entire life.

Or God forbid, you're where I found myself so many times, at the stage where you aren't even capable of getting up in the morning. Your stories have beaten you down so badly that you believe there isn't even a reason to get out of bed. You believe you literally have no value and add nothing to the world at large, so what's the point? Why bother getting up at all? There are so many different ways that our relationship to our stories can steal life from us. For some, you may be able to completely function in your thinking that you're unworthy, like I was. I simultaneously had ZERO confidence in myself, while having balls the size of a baby elephant.

I trained with the one and only Billy Blanks in LA to be one of only fifteen certified TaeBo instructors (able to teach his exercise creation combining martial arts and boxing). Hell, yeah, I did! I accomplished this, moved back to Toronto, and opened my own studio (the only sanctioned TaeBo Center outside of LA) with all the gumption of somebody who knew they'd be a huge success. But what was truly playing on a loop in the back of my head was: "Nobody will ever come to my classes cuz I'm not even going to be any good at it." But I did it. And it was great for three years before my self-sabotaging ways came along and destroyed it, along with my back.

Write books? Hell, yeah! But inside, I thought: "Your books won't even sell two thousand copies cuz nobody cares about you." Well, I tried to focus on writing to be able to help even one person, while also reminding myself every single day what a waste of money I was to my husband who was funding all of my schemes and dreams.

Buy a dilapidated 63-year-old marina on a lake that I'd spent one summer on in my entire life, even though I knew nothing about boats, or cottaging for that matter. WHY NOT?! I did that too. I'm now four seasons in and have yet to take a single paycheck, but as my girls like to remind me, since it's a seasonal business, I've not yet even been open for 365 days (at the time of writing this book. The year 2022 will be my year when I take a paycheck home!). So even though I've been doing this for four years and we haven't even done one full calendar year's worth of sales, I'm proud to say that I've already broken the million-dollar mark by selling gas, ice cream, and penny candy. This is working. This is being successful. The paycheck will come.

You want to know why it's successful compared to my other earlier ventures? There are a few reasons, so let me list them for you here:

1. I have released my attachment to and obsession with proving myself to others. Ever since I was little, I wanted to be good at something, to excel at something. I wanted my dad to notice me, to be proud of me the way he was organically proud of my brothers. I've been chasing the "I'll show you" moment since I was very young. I could list all the things I've done along the way in my attempt to win his love, but honestly, I no longer give power or energy to it, and I'd rather use my word count on shit that's going to help you, since this book is for YOU.

2. I have embraced, fully embraced, the knowing that it is absolutely true if the work you are passionate about and that you devote yourself to gives you joy, brings about change, or makes literally one person's life better, then guess what? Your work *does* have value. Your work is important to that person (or people).

3. I've let go of the traditional definition of success, and instead, I gauge success by what brings me joy. Not that building a business, a brand, or writing books shouldn't sometimes be stressful or feel daunting because, well, it's still work. But I constantly stop and take stock of the balance of stress vs. the joy and fulfillment I am feeling. And if the scales begin to tip too heavy toward it not being any fun at all, I stop and recalibrate.

4. I spend way less time on social media. Like way less fucking time. Because let's be blunt with each other, we all know that what we give our attention to we become. If we spend copious amounts of time daily comparing ourselves to the highlight reels of everybody else's lives, then we are going to inherently become less fulfilled and feel less grateful for our own beautifully complicated, challenging, but fulfilling lives.

Your Call to Action

This is my advice to you if you are having trouble deleting the negative tape that plays on a loop inside your head:

- Step away from social media. Delete it from your phone and take a legitimate hiatus.

- Seek out a therapist who deals specifically with the trauma you are combating. If you're unable to afford a therapist, then I encourage you to employ the resources at your disposal to find incredible therapists who have written books or who have podcasts dealing specifically what you're dealing with. *The Body Keeps the Score* by Bessel Van der Kolk is brilliant! And so is *What Happened to You* by Bruce D. Perry and Oprah Winfrey. These are great places to start if finances are an issue, like they have been for me so many times. Just because money is tight, doesn't mean you cannot start/continue to do the healing work.

- Hold yourself accountable. Tell somebody close to you, who you trust with your life, what you're going to do—whether it's quitting drinking or smoking, or if you're no longer going to over eat or under eat. Whatever physical crime you're committing against yourself as a means of punishing your body or as a coping mechanism to deal with your trauma. Let somebody you absolutely trust hold you accountable to actually STOP these toxic abusive behaviors for your own good.

- Meditate. I know I called it airy-fairy at the beginning of this book, but I don't fully believe that. I definitely don't think it's the be-all and end-all or the only way to heal yourself. But as somebody who has healed their traumas, I had to have an arsenal of tools to get the job done. It just can't be the only tool in your healing tool box. Nobody's out there building an entire house with just a hammer. But it can be a worthy one to add in and to employ. Join a meditation group (in person or online) to find a resource that is effective in teaching you how to meditate. I do all my meditations via apps.

One app I love and rely heavily on is "Awakenings with Iyanla Vanzant." She is a rock star spiritual leader who I adore. Check her out. I've also done online meditations with Linda Hall. Giovanni Dienstmann's "Letting Go of Regret" has had a profound effect on me releasing my guilt, shame, and regret of not doing more for the young child I was. Whoever you end up uncovering to guide you through your healing meditation journey, I strongly recommend that you put in some work to find your best teacher.

- Pray. Ask for guidance. Ask for direction from your spirit guides, angels, or whatever higher power you believe in. Tell them what you want, what you need, and where you want to go. Ask them to help you find the source that will take you there. It might be a workout, it might be an art or music class, it might be a trip . . . who knows what you specifically need to heal your wounds, but the Divine does. God does. Trust this, and ask for direction to your healing.

Once you've completed these calls to action, move on to this following exercise.

Exercise: The best way for you to release attachments to your old stories is to first acknowledge that you have some. Then, name them. Simply write out your stories. Bring them into the light. Take away their power by exposing them. And then decide to let them go.

It's really that straightforward of a task. You bring them to the surface, write them out, thank them for all the ways your stories have protected you from more harm, let them know that you no longer need them, then release them and send them packing. Like literally. Picture putting all your old stories in the basket of a hot air balloon, releasing the rope keeping the balloon tethered to land, and letting them all float away. Watch all your stories drift far, far away from you. Watch them until you can no longer see them on the horizon. Release those stories.

Now that you've decided to do that, you must commit to doing the rest of the work. All the work—not half of it, but all of it—until you get to the end where it no longer holds you prisoner in your own life.

Your life won't change overnight. You won't feel healed or as if you released your shit the one time you do the aforementioned exercises. These are meant to become rituals, habits that you develop daily so that you can truly release the shit that holds you back, that has tied you down and caused you to live your life half asleep, like half a person. Do the work, do it consistently, and the change will come. Trust me on this, because it did for me.

Forgiveness and the power
of letting go

We're in the final portion of the first section of this book that is going to guide you to living your best full life. We've dug deep and uncovered the things that happened to you in your past that currently have you stuck in a not so fulfilling, joyful, healthy present. But the great news is that all is not lost. There is still today. There is right now to get a hold of yourself and to choose to make a difference. To start living the life you've always wanted to live. Because, and let me be blunt, nobody is coming to your house to bring you the life you've always dreamed of. And I can assure you, the person (or people) who fucked you up in the first place isn't likely going to come to you on bended knee admitting they blew it, that they were cruel, wrong, unjust, and apologize. You might be one of the fortunate few who have received some type of acknowledgment or apology from the perpetrator, but in reality, the odds are heavily stacked against them ever owning their own participation in helping to fuck you up to this point in time. So now is the time to let that notion go. Let go of the expectation that they will behave the way you need them to so you can start to heal yourself. You must be able to acknowledge that you have to do the work to heal yourself regardless of their ownership in the tragedy. Because listen, if you want to have the life you've always dreamed of, you have to take back YOUR power. You have to start to show up in your life in the way that you want your life to BE. You have to elevate yourself in order to get the life you want. You cannot wait for them to give you permission by saying "sorry" or "I fucked up" or anything at all, quite frankly. You have to move on. You have to love yourself more than they did. You have to make a difference in your own life.

This is a tough part of healing. I know because I've had to do it too.

You will never, even in one million lifetimes, ever get the life you want and deserve if you leave that possibility in the hands of somebody else by waiting on them to release you with an apology. You have to move forward without that apology. You have to move forward without them taking ownership or them admitting that they wronged you. Most of us will never get that while we're six feet above ground. Often times the people who inflicted trauma on us don't believe they did anything wrong. They'll call us liars or say that the reason we were traumatized by something was because, fuck, we were just too sensitive. None of it is their fault.

The harsh reality in this part of healing your past is that it requires you to drop the victim story. Let go of the unrealistic expectations and get on with your life. I'm not sitting here all coldhearted denying that your trauma was actually traumatic. I'm not going to say you're not justified in your hurt, your anger, your desire for closure, or even in wanting revenge against the person who ruined your life. I'm just proposing, as somebody who had quite a few people I thought might be better off burned at a stake than allowed to continue to live their lives blissfully unaware of the way they tortured me, that it's time to let it all go. I spent countless days, nights, weeks, years really hating myself as a result of the way they abused me, and I wanted payback.

> *To forgive is to set a prisoner free and discover that*
> *the prisoner was you.*
> –Lewis B. Smedes

Because, as this quote says, the only person who is suffering and not getting out of life what they deserve is you.

And aren't you tired of it all?

Isn't the load too heavy to continue carrying?

Don't you want to soar?

Are you not ready to be free? Beautifully and wonderfully free the way God, the Divine, always wanted you to be?

I, for one, wholeheartedly believe in Karma, the afterworld, past lives, all the juicy stuff that gives me hope that this one life isn't "it." Although I will only ever be me once, and I won't remember me, my life, or any of it, I believe that it isn't all for nothing. That what comes our way isn't simply put on us for no good reason. What has helped me heal and let go of everything I've been through is the belief in the knowing, the real knowing, that if I help one person, then everything I endured, everything I went through was worth it.

I pray that you, too, can get to this point in your healing journey. I hope my experiences help guide you there. I share all that has happened to me with you not for pity, but for strength. To be made stronger by bringing it out of the shadows and into the light, where it no longer can cripple me into a heap of self-loathing with the momentary belief that the world might just be better off without me. I share my truth with you so that you will come to the very real understanding that you're not alone. And I share it with you in the hopes that if I can come out from under all of this to achieve and accomplish all that I have, which in my humble opinion is a great amount of goodness, then you can too.

But as always, if you're going to get to your place of healing, then I'm going to be completely and totally real with you. You absolutely can't wait for your abuser to own their shit. Regardless of where the other person is in the equation of your current pain that is holding back your one life experience, it's completely irrelevant as to your own power to be able to move forward. And in order to do this, you have to forgive them. You must. It will be difficult, believe me. I fully appreciate how hard it is because as I've shared with you many times, I've had to do it myself. And I'm not saying that the second you do this next exercise you're going to be magically healed. That all the heaviness inside of you is going to miraculously disappear. That you will shout these words, or cry them out, and instantly get to a place of peace. That would be crazy, and even though I love myself a little bit of crazy, giving you that false hope would not be cool. So instead, I will be honest with you and let you know that you will definitely experience some instant relief, but like me, you will likely need to make this a ritual. Something you say daily for at least thirty days. I encourage you also to put a prompt in your phone so that each and every day your phone will alert you to take a few minutes to find a quiet place to sit and chant these words for the next thirty days, three to five times each day. This is the start of forgiving, and it is an important and integral piece of getting to the point where you've truly and legitimately forgiven them so you can finally let it all go. Now, let's get down to the business of what your new thirty-day mantra is going to be.

Your Call to Action

Stand up, look in the mirror, and say: "I don't understand why you (insert their name) did _____ to me or why you don't see the pain it has caused me or why you don't even believe that what you did was wrong enough to apologize. But I want you to know that by holding you hostage, by not forgiving you, I'm actually holding myself back from being free. I release me. I release you. I forgive you. I've carried this long enough. It no longer serves me, and you no longer have power over me. So be it and so it is."

A book I truly love that was pivotal in me letting go of my past is *Let That Shit Go* written by an incredible human being, who I'm also proud to call a friend, Nina Purewal.

I think you can sense a pattern in this book I'm writing for you. I'm not so arrogant to think that I alone will help you get to the other side of your trauma. It takes a village to heal us, all these authors and experts are your village. We cannot heal ourselves alone, we need support, we need tools, and I am sharing with you the arsenal of tools that have truly helped me reclaim myself. They helped me come back home to live inside myself, to have the desire to want to be alive every single day, no matter how tough my days might get now. I no longer fantasize that death might be easier than life.

Forgiveness is not always easy. At times, it feels more painful than the wound we suffered, to forgive the one that inflicted it. And yet, there is no peace without forgiveness.

–Marianne Williamson

YOUR
PRESENT

Okay. I can appreciate that the first chunk of this book was pretty heavy. But it is always darkest before the light, right? We just spent hours (or days) scratching the scab of your wounds, and some of you might have had to put this book down to breathe. Or you may have ordered one or more of the books I suggested and you're now reading multiple books at once, hungry for the healing to begin in earnest. Ready to begin the first day of the rest of your life, so let's get to it!

Repairing your relationship with yourself

I don't know you the way you know you, but if you're anything like me, there is a tremendous amount of forgiveness you need to dish out toward yourself. For years and years, I truly blamed myself for every single thing that happened to me. I had myself convinced that I had created the perfect scenario for every single thing that was done to me. I was too friendly, too sexually suggestive (not exactly sure how since I was so little, but it absolutely had to be me). None of the other girls in my group of friends had boys hiding in their closets. None of the other girls in our apartment complex had been forced to have sex with somebody before they even knew what sex was, let alone even wanted it. Nobody else's step-grandfather was petting them at family functions. None of my friend's dads were telling them that the only really good thing about them was that they were pretty. Nobody else I knew was being called a slut by an entire grade of girls, even though she was only having sex with one person, her boyfriend. Nobody else I knew at church was being pulled into meetings with "women over them in the Lord" being told that their husbands had confessed lustful thoughts about them, so stop being you so their husbands would stop sinning. So, if it was only happening *to* me, then it had to be *because* of me. I mean there was literally nothing else to deduce from my childhood/teen years and early twenties. It was the one consistent thing about it all—I was at the epicenter of all the shortcomings of the men around me. Therefore, there was nothing more to discuss—the sure and absolute truth was that I brought it all upon myself.

And what began as things being done to me, quickly turned into me doing adult things with others long before I should have. I knew it was too soon, but I fully believed that it was all I was good for. I also believed that if I wanted anybody to actually like me and stay with me, then I better be extremely sexual with them. So, I ended up having sex with my high school boyfriend shortly after turning fifteen. Why wait to make sure he was going to be a good and kind boyfriend? He was cute and popular and new to the school. I simply wanted to make sure he'd stay. That he'd pick me. But I'm not sure how he would have made a great boyfriend when he came from a more fucked-up homelife than even I did. In our juvenile relationship, with these two disasters together, I found myself on the end of his yo-yo string in every way imaginable, all for male love, acceptance, and loyalty.

It wasn't until I became awake, like truly awake, to the ongoing trauma I was committing against myself when I was thirty-five that I got serious about healing myself all the way through. I had dabbled in healing myself through so many channels for a solid sixteen years, but I was never fully invested in it. I participated in The Forum (a.k.a. EST: an intensive

60-hour course over two weekends offered in the '70s and early '80s that tried to help attendees transform their lives by focusing on personal responsibility) with my young, soon-to-be husband at nineteen, then joined a non-denominational church for five years after the birth of my second daughter. When I hit thirty-two and there was one more infidelity that put the nail in my relationship with my husband, I turned my attention outside of my home and myself. I relied heavily on a gang of girlfriends for distraction, with lots of alcohol and clubbing, numbing it all away until the cracks became crevices and my marriage totally collapsed with a separation. You see, some might say that my husband's infidelities were all his fault, and granted, I will go to my grave saying that no matter how bad things get in a relationship, the brave and honorable thing to do is to leave if you're not getting what you emotionally need from your partner. You don't cheat. You simply don't. I mean cowards like my dad cheat, not gentle, respectful, loving men. They shouldn't cheat—but sometimes they do. Sometimes it has everything to do with them, but more often than not, if we sit quietly with ourselves and hold ourselves to the same standard of accountability at the same level we hold others to, we will come to the point of complete and utter honesty where we can take ownership of our part in the demise of a partnership. It's not the norm that relationship collapses are due to the actions of only one-half of it. I mean, obviously, abuse aside. We must be brutally honest with ourselves and look for our part, however small. It's just been my experience that in the same way it takes two to make an intimate relationship thrive and be healthy, the same applies to its demise. You'll never convince me otherwise. There is always something missing. The five love languages come to mind. For us it was affection. I was incapable of fully loving my husband. I mean, I loved him. I kept a beautiful home, stocked all his favorite foods, paid all our bills. I managed, cared for, and did the lion's share of parenting our three girls while he filmed. I did all the acts of love without fully giving my heart over to really loving him. Trusting him. Believing he'd stay or that he truly loved me. I spent tens of thousands of dollars, when we had them, to build my body into the bodies he cheated with. I thought for sure that if I carved myself into a dream woman, then he'd never stray again.

I dated and was obsessed with older men, who had the type of careers I either longed for myself or thought would provide great secure second marriage lifestyles (since ours was anything but!). I drank way too much. I smoked too much weed and too much hash. I partied, essentially redoing my teen years, except I was a mother of three in her early thirties.

None of it worked. Not one bit of it stuck. And for a full year of my life, I wandered around trying to put another square peg in the round hole of the partnership I longed for. There were countless empty dates, empty nights with the wrong people, and hollow conversations looking for a "better man" to make me whole. To make me happy. To, in the famous words of *Jerry Maguire*, have somebody "complete me."

Complete and utter bullshit.

That was my rock bottom.

Running away from everything that mattered to me caused me to become even MORE desperate for male approval. MORE insecure about what my worth in the world actually was. It was a complete and utterly beautiful disaster because hitting my rock bottom came in the form of me blowing out my lower back while teaching a class at my TaeBo Center in Toronto. I literally dropped like a stone, barely able to finish teaching. I then ended up in bed for ten straight days. Have you ever looked up what emotions are generally stored in the lower back? I have. Plenty. Because it just seemed so odd to me that a person who was so fit, so able bodied and teaching upward of ten of these classes each week would just blow out her back. But when I did some poking around, I uncovered that having lower back issues often goes hand in hand with intense feelings of low self-worth and a lack of self-acceptance, which is also accompanied by feelings of guilt, shame, and even sexual inadequacy or trauma. When I learned that I was like, "Yeah. It all makes sense now."

It was then I realized that if I didn't heal myself, I would destroy myself. And even though I had spent so much of my time feeling like I wasn't worthy of even being alive, I also had a strong desire to not only stay alive but to live a dynamic and brilliant huge life. There was no more time for fucking around. I didn't have any more time to hope that it would just all magically go away. The time to do the work was now. So, I began in earnest.

Your Call to Action

Exercise: Take a moment to reflect on your rock bottom. Write it down. Write it all down. Describe the sensation of hitting rock bottom, the moment when you knew you had hit it. And what you did once you were there.

The very first thing I had to do once I realized that I was getting further and further away from who I truly was inside—and who I wanted to become—was to start at the beginning of where and when it all went wrong. I found a therapist who dealt specifically with healing sexual trauma. I had to begin there because it was the foundation for all the other issues I was having. It was essentially the rock that my entire being was built on. I had developed coping mechanisms and created a protective layer around myself that made accessing myself impossible. If I couldn't even access me, how was anybody else ever supposed to? My biggest motivator to get well and to repair my relationship with myself was so that my shit didn't continue to roll downhill. It was a damn good thing I was all alone during this work that I was doing because it was dark, it was ugly, and it was painful. The best thing that could have happened to me was having countless days and nights of being alone, when Yannick had the girls and I could just weep for hours, sometimes days, to get it out. To process it all. To live it and release it.

It was—and is—the only way.

You have to go through your trauma, feel it, acknowledge it all the way in order to completely release its hold on you. Stuffing it down won't work. Acting like it's healed won't work. Denying that it's even there will absolutely without a doubt not work.

I know I'm like a broken record saying this to you, but I do not know what your story is. I've heard some unbelievably brutal, heart-wrenching stories from so many women who I've mentored, who have messaged me on various social media channels sharing their own journey with healing their trauma, and all I can say is that every single one of you reading this who has a story to tell and survived is a Goddess. Not all of us get to be so fortunate to live through our abuse. If you know somebody who didn't, I pray that their souls are long last at peace.

I believe that those of us whose mental and physical wounds didn't kill us have an obligation to ourselves, to our inner child, to fully heal. To show her that she is now free and safe to be happy. And to get to the point in our lives where we live without shame or blame or regret. We can only hold ourselves accountable for what we know now. We can't hold ourselves ransom for things we didn't know before. We could only heal to the point where we were emotionally ready to do so. It doesn't serve you one bit to say things like: "Oh, I wish I'd told somebody what _____ was doing to me." Or "I wish I had stood up to _____ when they would constantly call me stupid." Playing the blame game with yourself serves you not one bit. In fact, it keeps you perpetually stuck in the victim role and mindset. Because, my friend, if you're constantly living in your past, how the hell are you going to get into your present?

Newsflash: you will not.

It is impossible to live simultaneously in the past and in the present. It cannot be done. So, you must choose. No matter how lost you felt for however many years, or how much you believe that you hold no value and there's no reason for you to try to leave your past behind because you're entirely worthless (and you know this to be so because _____ told you as much your entire relationship with them), you can—and must—choose. Stop buying

It is impossible to live simultaneously in the past and in the present.

the lie that was told to you by somebody else. They had their own wounds and their own trauma and they dumped their shit on you. And you were either too small, too naive, or simply a trusting, pure, and loving soul who subconsciously accepted that shit as your truth.

But it isn't your truth. How people see you and how people treat you is THEIR TRUTH not YOURS. It never was yours. NONE OF IT. EVER.

So, let it go. Send it back to its rightful owner. Release it from you.

"Okay, Shantelle, sounds awesome. I'm just going to put your book down, click my heels three times, tell myself that there's no place like home was before I was wounded, and it should all just magically heal."

No. Not at all. I mean, it's sort of like that, but not exactly like that. Not entirely. The first thing to do to begin repairing your relationship with yourself is to do the next exercise. But this is a deep, DEEP exercise that you're going to be doing, so I highly recommend that you don't even think about beginning it until A) you're all alone, and B) you have the time in your schedule to do nothing at all afterward. And I mean nothing.

Like no errands, no phone calls, zero obligations for a good long while. I would actually love it if you would do this exercise when you can just stay in bed for the rest of your day. I'm serious. Connecting to your inner child is really that deep.

To show up for your inner child, you must first develop a relationship with her. Get reacquainted with your younger self. I remember the first time I ever spoke to my younger self was back in 2006. I was at a yoga fasting retreat in Desert Hot Springs, California. I knew nothing at all about inner child work up until that day. If you also have not ever heard about inner child work, it's (in layman's terms) when you explore the child of your subconscious, both in her positive and negative aspects. Some of the possible negative pieces of your childhood lying in your subconscious are tied to things that we talked about in the first section of this book: the self-doubt, the feeling of being worthless or unlovable might be lingering way in the back of your adult brain. The cool thing that I found about doing this sort of work was that not only did I get to deal with the negative elements of my childhood, but I also got to revisit and celebrate all that was beautiful in my early years. It was all shit that was a comforting thing to be able to call back to and look upon. I have

> To show up for your inner child, you must first develop a relationship with her.

to confess that the road to repairing my relationship with myself truly began in earnest when I was reconnected to the little girl I used to be. I was able to call her up and talk to her, to meet her when it all started to go sideways and thank her for being so brave, so strong, and so resilient. And to apologize to her for being unable to keep her safe. To tell her that I was sorry that I didn't know that I could tell somebody what happened to her, and that maybe if I had, the rest of what happened to her might never have happened at all. Once I was able to forgive myself for letting myself down, the other dominoes toward true healing began to fall.

I encourage you to explore the possibility that inner child work and healing is what you also might need in order to get on the path to finally healing your past so that you can live and thrive in your present. Because the reality is no matter how picture perfect our childhood may have been, based on the list of ways that our subconscious can experience trauma that I listed earlier, we all have a part of our experiences that live within us. And even though these things that happened to us might be many decades in our past, their effect on us still needs addressing. Some days they still rear their ugly head, and I have to step back and retrace some healing steps before I can continue forward.

But listen, this is not something to rush through and get it done quickly so you can keep reading this book or move to the next exercise. This inner child work requires that you take it seriously, and that you give yourself time to process everything that will likely come up. The more that has happened to you, the higher the likelihood that you're going to need more "down time" before continuing on. You might even want to break this work into three stages. Do one exercise a day, for three days. It all depends on what comes up for you with the first part of the work.

Resting is okay; quitting is not permitted.

Remember, repairing your relationship with yourself is a marathon not a sprint. You're not in a competition to get to the end of your healing journey, so take your time. Honor what shows up while you're doing this work. It's totally cool to step back and catch your breath. Just don't quit. You've spent enough time living outside yourself, putting yourself at the bottom of your to-do list—but no more. Resting is okay; quitting is not permitted. To be very clear, though, I want you to keep in mind that I'm not saying only do this exercise when you're "ready for it" because you know how I feel about that phrase, and how it's the lamest excuse in the world. I'm saying complete this exercise when you have the mental space and capacity to do it safely, and to complete it in one fell swoop, which means without disappearing for days on end, or stopping all together. A.k.a. pause, break it into digestible sections that work for where you are in this moment. Give yourself a timeline to complete it that makes emotional sense for you. For some, that might mean within two days; for others, it might be five to seven days. Whatever feels safest and best for you, do that. Because tying it all together, and doing it all at once makes the end result so much more powerful than if you half-ass it. And nothing about rebuilding your love affair with yourself should be done half-assed. I dare say the reason you picked up this book was because you've been cutting corners with yourself long enough. So, let's stop now, shall we? If you haven't yet made the vow to fully show up for your current self and your inner child, then I suggest here, at the halfway point in this book, is a great place to finally do it.

Alright . . . did you do it? Did you make the vow?

Awesome! Let's continue.

Your Call to Action

Exercise: Shut off all your distractions, get into a comfortable place, open your *WLYC* journal to an empty page, and start by writing a letter to your younger self. Introduce yourself to her; let her know that you are her at _____ years old now. Tell her what you do for a living. Then let her know you "remember when . . ." and share all the things you loved doing when you were little. Take a walk down memory lane writing out all the things you did together that made you so very, very happy.

Now take some time in silence to close your eyes with your hand on your heart and daydream about these joyous activities you used to participate in.

Now that you've reconnected with your younger self, I want you to turn to a blank page in your journal. In the very center of it, draw yourself when you were little. Now draw a large circle around her. The circle represents your life and boundaries prior to the traumatic event that shifted your reality. Everything on the outside of the circle is what cannot penetrate the safety of the circle. Inside the circle, I want you to write all around your younger self some of the activities you did that brought you joy. Then I want you to add words of love, encouragement, and support to your inner child within the circle. You can write things like "I love you" or "You're brilliant." Let her know "You are safe." Perhaps you want to let your inner child know how brave, cool, strong you think she is. Write everything you feel toward your inner child. All the beautiful things you remember about her before trauma came and changed it all. Only speak lovingly, gently, and kindly to her. Write until the words become a struggle.

Then once again I want you to close your journal, relax, place your hand on your heart, and maybe even close your eyes. Breathe in deeply through your nose, and exhale slowly and fully through your mouth. When you breathe in, say the words: "I'm worthy of love." As you exhale and empty your lungs, say, "I release the lie that I am unlovable." Do this for five to ten times. Do it slowly. Stopping and breathing deeply slows your heart rate, while signaling to your brain to relax.

Spending time with your inner child might be something that is required of you daily until you get to a place where you and she feel heard, forgiven, and healed. Perhaps screenshot or dog ear this exercise, as it is likely one that you will need to revisit many times.

Once I opened the door to communicating with my inner child in 2006, I continued to get closer to her with lots of various ways of uncovering how she was doing, and what she needed from me today. One of the most profound exercises I did was to meet her on what I like to call "neutral territory." I was told by the woman leading the session to go to my younger self's favorite place to be, which for me was the swimming pool at my apartment building. This was where I first spent a lot of time hanging out with little me, lying on the hot pavement drying off after hours of swimming. Talking. In our happy, safe place I was able to ask her questions like when was the first time she recalled feeling afraid. Unloved. Unworthy. Once I heard from my younger me, I hugged her. I cried while she cried. I apologized and told her that I loved her. That we were safe now, and that we could let all of that go.

Try calling your inner child forward. See if she will come meet with you. Spend time with her reliving the beautiful parts of your childhood. Find the joy. Find the parts of your childhood that were pure, good, and felt safe. Sit with her there. Witness her in innocent childhood. Ask her if you can join in the fun. Ask her if you can hold her hand and connect with her. Be with her. Feel her purity. Celebrate with her. Recall it all on a cellular level as the adult that you are. Then heal it.

It's fully within your power to move on—you simply need to be willing to put in the work. Like I've said before, you don't need to be able to afford a life coach or to go away to a retreat. You don't even need to leave your home. Now you can investigate online to locate an inner child healer who has courses available online. We will only go as far as we want to go in life, this includes in our healing work. Only you can repair the relationship you have with yourself. Nobody else can. Remember what I said about waiting for apologies in order to forgive, let go, and move on? Well, the same applies to getting back to yourself. Nobody else is going to make the reintroduction to you. All that you once were and all that you will be again. You have to do it. So I invite you to get on with it now. No time like the present!

Addressing your younger you, charting a new relationship of getting clear and right with her is a massive step in the right direction. But if you know anything at all about me by now, you know that I'm not a fan of lingering in the past. I'm all about uncovering it, laying it bare, addressing it, and healing it. Life is simultaneously too short and too long, so why bother wasting another minute living in your past life. It's time to step into the present and adopt new habits of behavior that have you honoring and prioritizing yourself. We need to begin the migration of bringing you into a present healthy loving relationship with you!

Let's get down to business.

As of today, I want you to commit to stop making excuses as to why you can't work out. Or why you can't eat better. Or get together with friends. Or find a better job. Or . . . whatever excuses you live with that you hold on to that identify you and have created this life you're currently living. I want you to let them go. Like not forgiving somebody for what they've done to you or making excuses to not build, create, and ultimately live the life you truly desire is the ultimate "fuck you" to who?

You guessed it.

YOU.

Now that we've identified what happened to you. And we addressed how forgiveness and releasing it are the first steps in moving through it. We also now know that the only person who is capable of truly holding you back is only you. It's only ever been you. Yes, yes, yes, that person did do that thing to you, just like the people did those things to me too. But I've not once, even in my most broken-down state, allowed anybody to steal my present from me. And I want the same for you. Don't let anybody do that to you either.

You are steering your own ship. You get to determine your route. You get to decide where you want to go and who you want to be now that you're all grown up. You don't need to seek permission anymore. No need to cower in the shadows of self-doubt any longer. You are a free being, capable of making your own choices. Nothing or nobody is holding you back.

Do you believe that?

This is a subject I am going to speak extremely briefly on, because I have no intimate experience with it. But I have many, many, many friends who have had to find the inner strength to come out as their authentic selves. They've had to find the courage, the words to let parents, loved ones, family members, friends, and society at large know that they are LGBTQIA+. They've had to love themselves extra for those who were, unimaginably, "intolerant" or "unwilling" to continue loving them once they were able to break through the archaic ideas of "normal" to express who they truly are deep down in their souls. This, as they've shared with me, is an incredibly lonely and painful time, made all the more lonely and painful when you know that the people you need to share your inner truth with are not going to be loving or accepting.

I cannot as a hetero woman, who identifies as female, know even for five seconds how difficult it is to have this be your reality, especially when you are very in tune with yourself and know from a young age who you truly are. But from my friends who have had to go on the journey of coming out, I understand how brave you are in freeing yourself from the chains that are placed on you from a society that has so much growing still left to do.

I also applaud with my whole being the mothers, the fathers, and the village who rally around young people who are trans. It is remarkable to me that these young beautiful beings are able to know this about themselves and have the bravery to share this reality with those in their lives. It is always my prayer that these children/youth/adults have the love, support, and people in their lives to help them release "the norms" and live authentically and freely as who they know they are within their spirit.

Loving ourselves wholly is a different journey for every single one of us. We all have our own demons to slay, our own hurdles to jump over, and our own truths to face. And the only way to get into a relationship with yourself where you can live authentically and love yourself without shame, guilt, or live with regret is to be willing to be brave. To be really honest with who you are, what you want and need to live this one life in a way that fulfills your entire being. Your life doesn't need to be perfect to be rich, it just needs to be true. The truer you live, the richer your life will be.

Because at the end of the day, you leave the same way you arrived: alone and naked. So while we're here, the most important thing we need to accomplish every single day of our lives is when we stand in front of the mirror, are we able to look our self in the eyes and confidently say that we're stepping into our power, and that nobody can stop us now? If not, then I want to encourage you to try again—and again and again—until you can. You might need to spend more time with your younger self and convince her to be brave. You might need to journal about all the feelings that come up the second you try to take that leap into your today by leaving your yesterdays behind. But whatever you do, my beautiful friend, don't stop here. Push through. I've been you. I've been stuck. I've slipped backward. It's all okay, and it will all be okay if you simply keep going forward. You can trust me on this. I've got you.

If it's important you'll find a way.
If it's not, you'll find an excuse.
–Ryan Blair

Uncovering hidden or lost passions

Getting reacquainted with your inner child and taking a walk down memory lane leads us perfectly to this next bit of coming into your present life. How revisiting your inner child helps with the here and now is because when you stepped back in time, you uncovered things about your younger you that filled your heart with happiness. You took yourself back to that place before the shit hit the fan where you had pure unbridled joy. For me it was in tap class or lying on the hot pavement feeling the sun suck the moisture out of my swimsuit and my skin after spending hours in the pool. Innocence found again. So as an adult trying to add back in some of the wonder of my childhood, I've brought back some of the things that brought me immense comfort, joy, and confidence. One of those things was writing.

Years ago, after reconnecting with my younger self, I began writing a book, a fiction book (which has yet to see the light of day . . . but if you know anything about me by now, you know that it will happen!). After writing my first novel, I turned my creative attention to writing TV show concepts, which I still dabble in today. From that I created a daily blog, and out of that came the beginning of my *WLYC* book series. And now here I am on book three. I always loved writing. It was a means of escape for me. I could create beautiful happy worlds or I could pour my soul out in poems. Whatever form my writing took, I recall it bringing me great joy. It was also one of the very first times in my life somebody ever told me that I was good at something. A teacher in Grade 7 told the school in an assembly that a story I had written was powerful and wise. Then in Grade 9, my English teacher often held my writing up, using it as an example with positive comments, words of encouragement, and good grades. It's no wonder that I returned to this outlet that throughout my darkest moments had given me so much confidence, purpose, and joy.

Once I started to gain some confidence on my journey of being a fully functioning, self-serving (in all the best ways) adult, I then began to expand my reach of finally doing things that I had always wanted to do. I took up horseback riding, which I loved and am so thankful that I was able to overcome my fear of horses by finally getting up on them. You see, one thing my mom passed down to me was this paralyzing fear of "breaking my neck or breaking my legs and never, ever being able to dance again." When I spoke of things that were perceived as dangerous, like skiing, watersports, or horseback riding, it was quickly shared that these were dangerous activities that should be avoided at all costs if I wanted to remain in one piece. With all that deep inside me, it was one of the things that I had to decide to overcome or "undo" and so I did. And it brought me a tremendous amount of joy. The other thing I started to do was participate in the other "dangerous" sports. I started skiing at nineteen, when my future father-in-law told me it was a requirement to date his son. Thankfully both father and son were ski instructor level skiers and taught me safely and quickly how to participate in that sport. Then came the watersports, much, much, much later in life, but come they eventually did! I learned to wakeboard at forty-nine. I did another "brave" thing that same summer when I purchased a marina, without knowing a damn thing about marinas. I did, however, know a great deal about people, especially kids, and after spending one summer on a lake for the first time in my entire life, I selfishly stocked said marina with all the comforts of city living. Vegan, vegetarian, and gluten-free foods were introduced so cottagers didn't need to get in their cars to go into town. I felt strongly that even when we're away from our lives in big cities, there are still some amenities that we like to have available to us, especially dietary ones, and I simply went for it. I jumped right off that cliff and am still having the time of my life, learning, growing, and bringing joy to hundreds of people all summer long. I skied "powder" snow for the first time in my life when I was fifty-one, and did it on double black diamond runs on Jackson Hole in Wyoming. Prior to that powder day in 2021, I had never attempted a single black diamond run, never mind a double! And in the summer of 2021, at the age of fifty-two, I learned to wake surf.

Do you see a pattern taking shape here?

> ## And a life where we don't stumble and fall and grow is no life at all.

I'm putting myself out there. At a point in time when so many people are "settling in to getting old," I'm living on the hairy edge, doing things that scare me, interest me, and excite me while I'm still capable of doing them. This is what living life out loud is all about.

It is about living wholly, authentically, and doing it regardless of fear of failure or the doubt that you're not actually strong enough, healthy enough, or brave enough to do it. You miss all the shots you don't take. That is the whole truth and nothing but the truth. If you haven't lived your life by the time your clock times out, you'll truly have nobody but yourself to blame.

But you might be thinking, "Well, what if I fail, Shantelle? Failure makes me want to die."

My guess is that somewhere along your journey of life you've failed before and you survived. I mean, obviously you did cuz you're reading this book!

Often times we sensationalize and dramatize all the "what ifs" in our minds to the point where we get ourselves tied up in knots and end up back on our couch without even trying. And a life where we don't stumble and fall and grow is no life at all. You have to show up for you. It is on you, baby, to feed your soul. If you don't treat that as an important priority of rounding out your spirit, then you truly cannot expect anybody else to do it for you. So often when we're dissatisfied in our own life and frustrated at our lack of emotional progress, or how we often don't live true to our own passions and dreams, we find it super easy to be critical of those who are. It's really easy to be jealous of somebody else seemingly living their best life, when you're

It's amazing how when you get busy living life, you no longer have time to watch and criticize others who live theirs.

not even living a half life. But really, who is to blame for that? Well, you are. The same way I was for not living my whole life before my healing work. I really must confess that when I was selling myself short and living from a place of lack due to my inability to move forward within myself, I had a lot more to bitch and moan and gossip about than I do now. It's amazing how when you get busy living life, you no longer have time to watch and criticize others who live theirs.

Your Call to Action

Exercise: Take some time to make a list of passions that if money were no object you would love to explore. It's sort of like a bucket list, but more in-depth. I want you to write down the things that you either let go of or have never even tried. Then I want you to write a date next to every single one. That date should be when you intend to attempt, learn, and complete that passion. (Keep it legal, people!)

Getting clear on what the fuck
you want and need

This is the section of the book where you take a long look in the mirror and ask, "What do I really want?" And "Am I truly living the life I want, where I want, in the job I want, with the person walking beside me who I truly want?" This is where the rubber is going to meet the road. We've laid bare all the circumstances that got you to where you are right now today, while reading this book.

Where are you? And is it where you want to be?

If not, what are you waiting for?

Are you living a life of priority? Or are you living a life that the "zombie you" walked into when you weren't whole? Ask yourself, "If I do the work, can I learn to be content and joyful in this current life I've built for myself? Or do I need a complete overhaul? Is my life in need of a renovation? Or is it a complete and utter gut job?"

When I ended my marriage back in late 2003, I was 1,000 percent confident that at the root of all my unhappiness, my discontent, and my bitterness was my marriage. Before I did all the work—years and years and years of it—I thought for sure that what I had was not what I wanted. So, let me be crystal clear here, friends: you can't skip the doing the work part and jump straight to the "getting clear on what the fuck you want and need." It doesn't work that way. And the reason it doesn't work that way is because the likelihood of you making changes in your life that will better serve you when you're coming from an unhealed place of trauma, disconnected from yourself, is very low. From my own experience, I would bet my last dollar that until you are healed, your life moves/choices/decisions will not be for your highest good.

Might I also bring your attention to the possibility that if you're feeling hopeless, lost, and uncertain, it could very well not even have anything to do with your relationship, or lack of one, or your kids, or the fact that you don't yet have them. It's also quite possible that you, like so many of us, are suffering from the stress of continuously living in an uncertain world. It is hard to feel sure that you're doing the right thing or that you're fulfilling your soul when at every turn there is the potential of another lockdown, another surge in cases, another round of closures. We are living in a time of unstable ground. We have no sure footing, anywhere. We're more anxious than we likely were before, and we take it out on those closest to us: ourselves first and our partners second. This is also something to keep in mind when you're lying awake at night wondering: "Is this as good as it gets?"

Before you kick your partner to the curb or throw the double bird to your employer or move to another state/province/country, please make sure you've done your homework by truly exploring your life from the

inside OUT. Is this the real state of your life? Remember
Or is this your life from the skewed toxic lens the two
of COVID trauma? And if you discover that Ps: have
your discontent has nothing whatsoever to do perspective
with the pandemic we're now living with, then and be
I implore you to do the work. There is a huge prepared.
difference between making excuses as to why
you won't move in life and jumping off the cliff without a life jacket
knowing you can't swim. Remember the two Ps: have perspective and
be prepared.

Got it?

Yes?

Good.

Carrying on. If you're not beginning on your journey of self-discovery
and healing, but my book is the cherry on top of the work that you've
previously done and you feel ready to take yourself and your life to the
next level, let me share with you what helped me get to where I am today.
Grateful to be alive. Grateful to have my marriage, my daughters, and
now a grandson.

I knew that what I needed in my life was a partner who would hear me
when I spoke. Not just feign hearing me, but truly listen to my needs,
my wishes, my dreams, everything. I grew up not being heard by my
primary male relationship, so I really needed Yannick to show up for me

in this way. I also came to learn that I wanted a lot of personal freedom. I wanted to have my own identity that was separate from being a wife and mother. It wasn't that I didn't love my role as wife and mother, but I really wanted to be known as my own person, with my own thoughts, ideas, ambitions, and achievements.

It is extremely beneficial for me to do things that are entirely mine. For example, writing these books. It is all me, with no other input from the key relationships in my life. I've discovered that I crave autonomy in my intimate relationship. Luckily, I'm married to a person who is not insecure or controlling and very easily gives me the space to be "alone" in our marriage and to do my own thing. Even when I was like, "Let's buy the marina!" His response was: "No, thank you. I don't want another job." It wasn't: "No, I don't want to do that and therefore, you are not allowed to do it either." It was very clear that he wasn't interested in running it one little bit, but he would support me and back me if it was something I truly wanted to do. And now here we are four summers later with an extremely successful marina on our lake. Both of us are happy.

I also realized that I really needed him to initiate intimacy with me. Because I didn't have a father who wanted to be close to me, it really helps my inner child feel loved and wanted, instead of neglected and unwanted, when Yannick is affectionate or says kind, loving words to me first. It ignites the love hormone in my brain, and I instantly feel calm and safe.

These are just a few examples of how I learned to uncover what my intimate wants and needs are in my primary relationship. With uncovering what I needed emotionally in my relationship, it became easier to unlock what I truly needed sexually as well. It always amazed me that as a sexual abuse survivor, I still had an appetite and desire for sex. I've read many cases where sexual assault/rape victims have a block with their own desires to be sexually connected with others. I have not struggled with my own enjoyment of sex or my passion for it. But one thing I did suffer from was an intense feeling of guilt post orgasm. It didn't matter if orgasm was brought on through masturbation or intercourse, my emotional reaction to it was always the same. Guilt. Shame. One or the other, and often both. I didn't speak of it to Yannick for like forever. It wasn't until after we reconciled and I came clean on everything else that had happened to me that I was able to begin to open up about how I would always feel bad for enjoying sex. It wasn't until almost two decades together, with a loving, sensitive, invested partner that I was able to be this vulnerable with him. And again, the only reason I was able to "go there" in conversation with the man who had walked beside me for all those years, the man I made a family with, was from doing my own inner work and healing.

And let's be frank here, ladies, you don't even have to be somebody who has healed from sexual trauma to have a bizarre relationship with sex, for fuck's sake, you might only need to simply be a woman who was raised in a household where sex was taboo, or worse, it was portrayed as being evil, bad, wrong, or dirty. So many parents raise their daughters with the garbage that women who enjoy sex are less than women who do not. That women who glean pleasure, joy, and satisfaction from a healthy sex life should be ashamed.

This is complete and utter bullshit. This is the patriarch hard at work trying to yield sex like a weapon over women as a way to control us, and to raise women to believe that men control sex—which is a lie! Which by this point in time of your life I pray you have come to this realization too. That it is your God-given right to be sexual. To have as many sexual partners as you desire, as long as they aren't somebody else's current sexual partner—this is where I draw a hard line, ladies. If they're already in somebody else's bed, move along, go get your rocks off with somebody who is available. As many available somebodies that feed your soul . . . and your vag.

If you are somebody who has intense guilt, shame, and anxiety around sex, then I encourage you to really explore the whys of it. Don't live a life void of sexual pleasure, because like I've always told my girls, "Life is tough and shitty and so often mundane that the one thing you want to make sure you always have access to is GREAT sex." When everything else is going wrong, knowing that you can get thirty minutes of great sex—or hours if you're Sting and Trudie—is something to hold on to.

I could go on and on about how I got in touch with the other ones, but it would literally take up the rest of the book, and since I already touched on what I did to reclaim and ignite my hidden and lost passions,

I think I'll dedicate the rest of this section of the book to you. So please, if you have hang-ups around honoring, feeding, and fulfilling your own (legal) sexual desires, take this as your wake-up call to get to access the sex you deserve. Do not waste another minute being disconnected from your bodily desires and settling for mediocre sex. Get direction from a sex therapist or a great book and get busy! You won't regret unleashing your inner Goddess—neither will your partner!

Your Call to Action

Exercise: Time to grab your *WLYC* journal and describe your dream life. What would it look like if NO was not an option? Don't sensor yourself. Don't edit. Write in a total stream of consciousness about what you want and need that you're lacking in your current life setup. If you have the time, create a vision board. I'm not normally a fan of these cuz it sort of removes the responsibility from you working at bringing about the change you want to see in your life and puts it into the realm of airy-fairy. But it can also help us hone in and get extremely clear on what it is we require to live whole fulfilling lives.

In this dream life exercise include what an ideal sex life looks like to you. Are you with the partner you really desire? Are you currently in a hetero relationship but really desire a same-sex partnership? If so, how do you go about getting that? Are you having enough sex? If not, how often would be perfect for you? Get really real about what a satisfying sexual life looks like to you and for you. No time like the present to get everything you want, need, and desire.

Remember that nobody can make you feel unloved, unworthy, unwanted, or less than in any way without your permission. You must be your own advocate, which is extremely challenging when you're recovering from a trauma, because the harsh reality about that is when this is your reality, you have something of a disconnection to others. Trauma creates what I like to call "lone wolf syndrome" where the person who is still ensnared in it believes that they're completely alone, isolated, the only one of their kind, so to speak. So, you build an existence where you come to rely solely on yourself and you don't let anyone into your life because 1) why bother since you can't trust them anyway, and 2) they'll never fully understand you. This leads me to the next point in making the most of your present life, which is to get to a place where you know the value of setting up your emotional parameters, otherwise known as setting boundaries.

Remember that nobody can make you feel unloved, unworthy, unwanted, or less than in any way without your permission.

Setting boundaries

Oh man, this for me is such a juicy topic when it comes to loving oneself with the fierceness of a lioness, because let's be blunt, ladies, most of us suck at setting boundaries with others. And the people we are likely to suck at it the worst with are our family members, specifically our parents. For the longest time, while I was walking around unhealed and completely locked and tethered to the ground by complete fear, I thought I had to always love and respect my parents. It is what I owed them for, well, being my parents. It wasn't until I understood that I was allowed to not only disagree with them, but I was also entitled to take breaks if it felt like that's what I needed to do for my emotional health that I healed. Sometimes my stepping away was steeped in drama. But now when I look back on it with a clear and HEALED (I know I say this a lot, but I say it cuz it makes a fucking world of difference) soul, I was able to come to a place of ownership for my part in the breakdown of our relationship. I was finally able to reconnect and have a true authentic relationship. I've had to do this with both my parents at various times in my life. Obviously, I had to do it with my father for longer, like many, many years of having no communication with him until he was ready to own his shit. Once he got to a place where he could take ownership and apologize from a sincere and humble heart, we were able to mend our fractured relationship and forge a new one.

Not all difficult relationships in our lives turn out this way. Sometimes we never get the opportunity to experience a key important relationship in a healthy way. And as painful as that is to acknowledge and come to grips with, we must also ask ourselves if letting it go is actually a better emotional parameter than constantly allowing somebody to hurt us. I dare say, it is much more painful to keep a wound open and festering than it is to get the stitches and go through the pain of healing it. Then it's over and you can move on.

We often let ourselves down by not establishing any healthy boundaries with work. As somebody who employs twenty-one people, I have to make sure that I don't take advantage of their willingness to work harder, longer, and later. I find I'm constantly checking myself to ask if their offer of doing more is really necessary. Does it pertain to a task that can wait until tomorrow? Stuff like that. We need to be mindful of what is essential to doing your job excellently, and what is you giving too much because you might be the sort of person who is constantly looking for approval. Maybe you're after acknowledgment to make up for being told you were lazy as a child or that you weren't smart. Anything really. Often times we're unable to erect healthy boundaries in our work because so often in our modern society we hear directly, or indirectly, how disposable we are. How there were hundreds of candidates for your job. I've watched my girls suffer through legitimately inhumane working conditions because the person who was their boss reminded them daily that if they didn't want to work an 18-hour shift, causing their hourly wage to be cut in half they could easily get somebody else who would actually do the job for free.

This is how some employers speak to their employees out there in the world. And you might be one of those employees truly fearing for their livelihood. In a time when so many of our jobs are being done by technology, it's no wonder intelligent, sensible people are not setting boundaries in the workplace. Creating healthy boundaries at work might involve ensuring that you're free and safe to do your job without being sexually harassed.

There are all sorts of reasons why and where you might need to establish boundaries to ensure that you're putting your mental health as a top priority. Often, if you don't communicate clearly to those around you what your emotional parameters are, you can wind up burned out from people pleasing or you can end up being taken advantage of and feel used. You see it in friendships. All. The. Time. I have a successful, intelligent friend who has run her own seven-figure business for years. She loaned a friend cash to help them also start their own business. But there was no contract, because why would they need one for helping a friend get to where you are in life by supporting them with a loan? That is until

Listen to what your inner voice is telling you to do.

said "friend" denies you ever loaned them any money, and there is no business to speak of. This is an extreme example of friends taking advantage; some are just fucking their friend's husbands. I kid. I mean, not really, this also happens all day, every day. (Let it be stated for the record that I don't personally know of anybody's friend who has fucked their husband.) Boundaries get set when we trust ourselves and our instincts. Don't ignore that gut feeling that tells you to put some distance between you and _____.

Listen to what your inner voice is telling you to do. Establishing boundaries plays an essential part in our mental health and overall well-being. And I know as a little person you didn't have the capability or the language to demand respect for yourself, nor did you know the importance of protecting and guarding yourself the way you do now. If, like me, you've spent an entire life searching for acceptance, setting boundaries can be really hard for you because you want to fit in and to be liked. If you let too much slide with other people, then try these following steps, based on which ones apply to where you're lacking a clearly defined boundary.

Your Call to Action

- If you're at home with a new baby and are feeling over-whelmed (like you're doing the lion's share of the work), before you have the chance to get bitter about it, ask your parenting partner to sit down and have a conversation when you're feeling calm and able to bring up your needs in a way that you know you'll be heard. Then tell your partner that you need more support. This might mean that you'd like them to do the last night time feed so you can get to bed earlier because you need to do the middle of the night feed. Or you might need your parenting partner to take the baby for a walk for an hour each day to give you a chance to catch your breath. Nap. Shower. Cry. Whatever you need the time for. The point is you're asking for what you need. Finding your voice early on in your mothering journey will help you feel more supported and less frustrated by the daunting new role you're fulfilling.

- In a romantic relationship, you may feel like your partner is smothering you, and you're afraid if you ask for space they'll take it as a sign that you want to end things. To be clear that this is not what you want, make a plan with your lover where once every two weeks you both go out and do your own thing with friends. And if you don't live together perhaps it looks like you don't see each other every single night of the week, maybe you take hump day off. For some, your needs and reasons for boundaries might be a tad more urgent and might be required to add more balance in the relationship. If you feel that you're bordering on being in a toxic abusive situation, then a boundary might not be enough space for you to ensure that you're honoring yourself above your partner. You might find you're at the point where you actually need to end the relationship. This is something you need to work out while exploring the new notion of implementing boundaries in your life.

• In your work relationship, maybe you have a boss who asks you to change your shift, stay later, or change your days off with no notice. A great way to establish a boundary in this situation is to have a talk with your employer and tell them that you often have plans for the hours that you're not scheduled and being asked with no notice to make changes to your work schedule has seriously negative impacts on the rest of your life. Let them know that you would appreciate going forward that they ask for any changes to your work schedule at least one week in advance.

- If you have kids, it's a good idea to teach them young about boundaries, so they come to understand that you're not just Mom, you're your own person who requires your autonomy. This usually presents itself in first letting children know that you have the expectation that they don't simply barge into your room, but rather they knock and wait for permission to come in. What this does in turn is it teaches your child(ren) that having limits and boundaries for oneself is not only an okay thing to do for themselves, but it's essential.

I could easily go on, but you get the picture. These are some easy examples of what setting a healthy boundary looks like. The key to setting a healthy boundary in any of your relationships is to: 1) Define within yourself where you feel you need to add some boundaries in order to experience more consistent mental health.

2) Once you're clear on where there is a need for a boundary, establish who the boundary needs to be communicated to. If you're nervous about potential conflict, you might find it helpful to first jot down your thoughts and rehearse saying it out loud to yourself in a mirror so you get comfortable with expressing your needs out loud, rather than simply in your head. I swear, one of our girls will be telling us about a situation she's embroiled in with somebody, and she'll say, "And then I was like_____" and it sounds so strong, so confident, so assured that we ask her if she really said that. And 90 percent of the time, she'll reply with, "No, but I thought it." My lovelies, it does you absolutely no good to only think about speaking your truth and setting up boundaries. You have to actually do it. Say what you mean—mean what you say.

3) Don't be like me and take the long way to tell a short story. There is no need for you to over explain your reasons as to why you are setting up the new boundary with them. The simple fact is that you are. No need to make a mountain out of a molehill, my friend. It is what it is. You are asking that this new emotional parameter be respected and that's that. Case closed. It's nonnegotiable. Not open for debate or interpretation.

It's not likely that the person you're setting this new boundary with will get onboard with it right away, but hopefully they will. I always lean toward the side of having great faith in the goodness of humanity and their willingness to be kind, caring, and genuine in their dealings with me. Sometimes I'm disappointed; but often I find that my interactions with others go how I intend them to, peacefully, with both sides feeling important and respected. It's my wish that you, too, will experience the peace of mutual respect in all your intimate relationships. You're well on your way now that you're a boundary-setting Queen!

Severing the unhealthy ties
that bind you

Examining your need for boundaries lands us smack dab here. If you shared your need for emotional parameters with others and they aren't respecting them, then guess what time it is? It's move the fuck along time! It's not always necessary to completely sever ties with somebody who you're not seeing eye to eye with. Like in the case of my mom and me (both extremely strong and opinionated women), you might just require a break from each other to grow, evolve, and come to the understanding that you don't always have to agree in order to love each other. If you want to clean house in your relationships, then do some deep soul work. Not everybody who is around you right now will be able to, or is necessary, to remain once you come through to the other side of this deep healing you're embarking on. Once we've healed, we're a completely different person than we were unhealed. We see life through a different lens. We no longer sell ourselves short or accept mediocrity from ourselves or the people we're spending our time with. Our threshold for bullshit goes way, way, way down. The minute you start digging deep and establishing healthy boundaries for yourself in your relationships, you might find that the person you're dating is actually toxic. Or the job that made you feel like you are living in hell every single day really is awful, and it has nothing to do with you. Your instincts were correct all along.

So often children of trauma don't trust anything their instincts are trying to tell them. They're shut off from hearing themselves, their guides, and their angels. They don't see signs. They often do not engage with their spirit at all. Therefore, it really is no surprise that more often than not they're engaged in abusive relationships or in toxic behavior, such as addiction. And I hate to jump on the bandwagon of hatred for the mainstream media, but I mean, come on, it really isn't doing us any favors. It is absolutely not set up to support us. A lot of shows present rich, famous, and sexy people eating, drinking, and shopping to excess for "happiness!" Feeling depressed? We're given so many mixed messages about how to quickly treat it. Like just pop this magic little pill. Hey, it might actually make you suicidal, but hell, you won't know until you give it a try! We're constantly bombarded with unhelpful information on how to numb our true feelings. We're not educated about how to deal with them or guided on how to get to the bottom of WHY WE FEEL THE WAY WE FEEL.

Don't ask.

Don't deal.

Just numb.

Numb it out with food, with sex, with shopping, with alcohol or drugs, with too much exercise or no exercise, with reality TV or social media.

Just get distracted. The more distracted you are, the less pain you feel.

Really?

Is that so?

I mean, countless quacks and billion-dollar corporations (hello, social media) would love for all of us to believe it. But if it were really the way to internal joy, fulfillment, and happiness, then why is suicide at its highest rate ever? In Canada, more than ten people die by suicide every single day! In the United States, someone dies by suicide every eleven minutes! And countless more attempt it or contemplate it. If all these "distracting" activities, that often create more distance between us as human beings, were actually better for us, then why are so many of us more lonely, more lost, more obese, and more depressed than ever before? So, when I talk about severing the unhealthy ties that bind you, I'm talking about you getting really, really honest with yourself and removing things in your life that you know without a shadow of a doubt are robbing you of any opportunity to be happy.

For me, I uncovered one activity that made me really feel gross when I did it: gossip. Gossiping made me feel uncool and like a shitty person. So, it is my commitment every single day to speak kindly about people. To speak about others without judgment. To say things about them that I would only ever say to their face. This has helped me cut way down on the shit that comes out of my mouth. Because let's face it, gossiping is fun, right? It's totally harmless. It's just talking with your friends or your partner. The other person never even knows that you're gossiping about them. *So harmless.*

No, it's actually not. Gossiping is mean. It's not only detrimental to the person you are gossiping about (God forbid they should ever hear it), but also to YOU! You're not naive—every single person reading this has absolutely been on the receiving end of gossip, and I'm sure you can recall exactly how you felt. It made you feel small, insecure, targeted, and it absolutely without a doubt made you uncomfortable to be in the same room, or even in the proximity of those who were gossiping about you. But what does participating in gossip about others do to you? Well, let's be blunt here, shall we; the first issue with being a gossip is that it's distracting you from doing more productive things with your time, your day, your life. And remember what we're after is to get you focused on taking the utmost care of yourself,

Commit to removing gossip from your life. It will help you feel like a better human being, trust me.

loving yourself, and building a better healthier life for yourself. Wasting time on a negative activity is a big energy sucker. There is also the fear and insecurity it brings up within you while you're doing it. I mean, I know whenever the shit is rolling off my tongue, I'm already thinking, "Wow, do these people I'm gossiping with about _____, gossip about me when I'm not with them?" It's a natural human reaction to have when trash talking somebody else you're supposed to respect, be friends with, or damn, love. So do like me and commit yourself to removing this unhealthy habit from your life, because let's be honest with one another, do you ever actually feel better when you're gossiping?

No. No, you do not.

I know I never ever did, and I never do. Which is why I work very hard to not gossip. Now let's be clear, there is a difference in gossiping with your partner or friends to sharing information about how your day went or how somebody behaved directly to you in a way that upset you. Gossip is different. It's sharing rumors, information or misinformation that is often negative and unfounded.

I mean, why are any of us having speculative conversations behind the backs of others? Commit to removing gossip from your life. It will help you feel like a better human being, trust me.

Another unhealthy practice that you might engage in, if you're anything at all like me, is eating when in pain. Some friends of mine have no appetite when they're in the middle of an emotionally trying time. I have the exact opposite reaction. The other negative part about my unhealthy tie to food when struggling emotionally is that I don't exactly make the healthiest food choices. It's not like I'm binge eating blueberries and broccoli. No, ma'am, without fail I'm eating chips, fried foods, and drinking alcohol. This self-sabotaging pattern of mine was really beginning to take its toll on me physically. My cholesterol was through the roof. I was having sleep issues. And non-nutritious foods don't exactly help with mood. So needless to say that when I now am going through an emotionally difficult time, I'm mindful to not stuff my feelings down with food.

This change did not come easily to me. And I'd love to sit here and tell you that I've completely broken this pattern in my life, but that's not the case. I am much more aware and am so much better at being organized around food, since one of the things I've discovered about me is that when I'm busy, I don't make proper nutrition a priority. Now, let's be clear here, I'm talking "proper nutrition" not dieting. I'm saying for our mental well-being, our ability to focus, and to take the best care of ourselves and others who rely on us we need to eat well. This is not the same thing as counting calories or denying yourself access to all foods in order to hit some number that somebody "out there" has told you will give you value. That number will make you acceptable in social circles, in your place of employment, blah-blah-blah. The body terrorism is alive and well in us women. I mean it's hard for it not to be since it's been put on us for the last two hundred years.

You've been to a museum. You've seen the art in person and online where women who had full round bellies and full heavy breasts were once celebrated. Women with these shapes were desired, coveted, and thought to be exquisite. What happened to her? Where did that beautiful womanly shape go? And why are we women working so damn hard to lose all our curves—only to then add them back through surgery? Breast implants come to mind. When did it become the norm to be straight up and down with washboard abs? And why is it that any woman who isn't shaped in this way is abnormal?

Listen, I'm not telling you to judge women who are naturally thin or who don't have naturally full breasts and opt for implants. Not at all. Because well, then, I'd be a hypocrite, wouldn't I be? I'm questioning why a curvaceous woman can't be accepted for her natural build. Why a naturally thin woman can't do with her body what she wants to in order to feel feminine and beautiful and complete. If you know anything at all about me, you know I'm famous for saying all the time: "What somebody does to make themselves happy—if it's not hurting anybody—is totally cool with me. It's not my business." And I mean that. I especially, passionately, believe that about women and their bodies, their shapes, their weight, and how they like to dress. None of our business. But for many of us, we can't help ourselves. We can't not be judgey of someone else's body. We judge whether we think theirs is better (fitter, smaller, stronger) than ours or worse (heavier, thicker, less toned) than ours. We have an opinion and we judge. Body shaming others is often times rooted in envy or jealousy over what we perceive—thanks to what society has told us for years—is the ideal body for one to have. So, my friends, this section is a good time to get real with yourself about why you struggle with feeling jealous of someone else's body or why another's body might "disgust" you.

Dieting? Do you eat carefully because you want to live a healthy life—as best as one can—by eliminating certain foods because you see that as a way to be proactive for your health? If this is your reason, then I say: AMEN! Yes. Food is medicine. But if you eliminate, avoid, or restrict food in order to hit a number on a scale, that's a whole other kettle of fish that needs addressing. This sort of eating can be the root of a much larger issue. I invite you to explore your reason why you're treating yourself in this way. I need you to examine why you do the things you do to your body.

When I'm living in a way that doesn't honor me by working too many hours and not sleeping during optimal sleep hours (often noted to be between 10 p.m. and 5 a.m.), I let other things that are good for me slide too, such as healthy eating and exercise. And this quickly becomes a vicious circle that you, too, might be familiar with. When I'm tired, I order in. When I order in, I order comfort foods, not whole, healthy ones. Then I also overeat because the portions are usually huge and well, I hate wasting food. If you're like me, you grew up hearing that there are plenty of starving people around the world, so you have to eat all the food on your plate. We all have so many stories that have been put on us by our parents, our friends, or our partners. In fact, eating disorders affect both boys and girls, so keep a close eye on your kids. Often times, it's when we start to become sexual that we begin to become incredibly harsh and cruel to our beautiful perfect bodies. At the end of the day, only you can stop body terrorism at its source by no longer committing it against yourself. And when you stop putting these barbaric expectations on yourself, it's amazing how you stop holding them over other women too.

Two great resources for healing your relationship to your body and to food are: *The Body Is Not an Apology*, which I mentioned earlier, and *The F*ck It Diet* by Caroline Dooner. Both were game changers for me. As I shared, healing my relationship to food and my body isn't complete, but I'm in the best place of my entire life in both areas. I'm still doing the work at healing this part of me, which as a former bulimic isn't always a straight line.

Because here's the thing about healing oneself, it's not the end of you ever feeling or struggling. Not by a long shot. So those of you who are reading this hoping for a magic bullet that will keep you from ever feeling pain, anguish, or disappointment toward yourself or life, should put this book down now. There is no point in time in life where you will live in endless bliss. But what I do hope you receive from my book is:

1) The comfort in knowing that you are not alone, not ever.

2) There are things you can deal with and remove in your life that will without a shadow of doubt give you relief from your pain and your demons. I know it because it did for me.

3) You will collect tools to use so that the dark times will be less painful

> There is no perfection in healing– there is only learning, undoing, and being better than you were the day before.

and will last for shorter periods of time.

Doing the work of healing your "self" and bringing you back to your "self" is not an exercise in getting it perfect. There is no perfection in healing—there is only learning, undoing, and being better than you were the day before. It's not like achieving a grade of "better," but actually mentally, emotionally, and physically feeling better. The goal here is to cut the cords to the things you know are robbing you from living a peace-filled life. None of us were born to suffer through life. Life is meant to be a gift. And no matter what you've endured, there is truly no reason why you cannot get to that place in your life where you can access the joy that is free and available to all. You have to want it—and you have to commit to getting it.

Another universal classic unhealthy habit that many people are tied to is not showing up for themselves in the way of taking care of their bodies. Again, I hate to sound like a broken record, but this can be via abusing alcohol, drugs, food (too much or too little), and by being sedentary. The saying "if you don't use it, you lose it" applies to the strength of our physical body in every single way. If you don't exercise, guess what? Sooner rather than later, you won't be able to open a jar of pickles, which might be cute when you live with someone who will open the jars for you, but what about if after some self-healing work, you kick your partner to the curb. Who is going to open those jars now?

I'm obviously being sarcastic and sassy here. But not entirely. The reality is if we don't take care of our one body starting right now, then there's no way that this body is going to be able to carry you through your one life. I'm not saying you need to start training for a marathon tomorrow, but hey, you might want to. I'm simply saying that if you want to be able to bend over and tie your shoes for your entire life you must stop taking your body for granted and start exercising to make her strong.

Like I've said before, I don't know your past, so I don't know what health costing habits you're in a negative pattern of behavior with. It might be that you don't believe you have value or worth, so you're promiscuous. Now before you jump down my throat, I'm not saying that having a robust sex life that might involve many sexual partners is not how women should behave; remember, I'm the one who encouraged you to uncover your authentic sexual self. I happen to think that it's hypocritical that men having many lovers automatically makes them excellent lovers. Whereas women who have had a healthy number of lovers would be labeled a slut. Do. Not. Even. Get. Me. Started. On. The. Patriarchal. Bullshit. That. That. Is.

No, that's not what I mean by this statement at all. What I am asking you to do is to check in with yourself regarding your sex life is whether or not you have negative feelings during or after sex. Do you feel guilt, shame, fear, or insecure? Is the way you have sex performative? Do you feel yourself doing things only because you think it will bring your partner pleasure? Are you doing things that you don't want to be doing sexually just to feel loved? Are you acting instead of engaging in the act of love making? Do you even enjoy sex? These are all good questions to ask yourself as you explore what a healthy sex life is for you. And only you know in your heart if you are using sex as a way to feel wanted, needed, adored, or appreciated.

My lovelies, this section could most likely make up an entire book all on its own because quite honestly we humans are complex beings. We all carry different stories and have been raised with a range of values and ideals, shoulds and should nots, that we're trying to reconcile within ourselves and with those we're in relationships with. It might seem impossible to list all the potential unhealthy patterns that you might be attached to that need severing. Yours might be straightforward and obvious. You might already know you're in a relationship with somebody who is wonderful, kind, thoughtful and loving, but they're just not the best partner for you, and it's time to move along.

Or maybe you know that you're locked in with a group of friends that you've outgrown. That you love, but they don't provide the energy you need in your life anymore. I've had to do it many times with friends. The expression "people come into your life for a reason, a season, or a lifetime" is no joke. It's never easy to walk away from a relationship, especially the longer you've been in it. When we make connections to people, we have no idea how long they will be with us. None of us have a crystal ball into how a friendship that starts out healthy, light, and fun might end up bringing out the worst in you. But what we do know for certain, if we're paying attention, is that once a relationship starts to take more from you than it gives you, it's time to sever that tie.

Your Call to Action

Exercise: Spend some time quietly reflecting on your patterns of behavior. In your *WLYC* journal, create two columns: one positive (for behaviors that serve your highest good) and one negative (for patterns that don't serve you at all).

I want you to then write out every single habit that you have that is toxic. And beside each one, I want you to write your plan to eradicate it from your life and why, along with a date when you will cut the tie to it. You must be serious and you must be committed. You can't break a destructive habit by giving yourself an out by telling your brain, "Okay I'm going to TRY to stop drinking myself to sleep every night." No. You need to commit to the act: "I AM NO LONGER DOING _____." As my coach Leisse Wilcox told me: "Your brain doesn't understand try."

A good way to reinforce positive thoughts and patterns is to take a second to give yourself a high five when you go against your nature or pattern of behavior by conducting yourself differently. Literally congratulate yourself. Take the time to acknowledge it. One of my daughters has a victory jar and every time she behaves the opposite of how she used to, she puts a buck in it; and at the end of every month, she uses the money for a meal out or on a piece of clothing. She treats and rewards herself for breaking the cycle, which I happen to think is brilliant. Get that dopamine connected to the positive choice and literally create a feel-good pattern!

Letting go of anything, even when it's something we know isn't serving us, isn't easy. Be patient and kind with yourself as you go through this letting go process. Remember, it never serves you to get upset when it's time to let go. Don't blame yourself for not knowing better. Or for allowing unhealthy habits and patterns to have a foothold on you and your beautiful spirit for so long. Be gentle with yourself and remind yourself that you can only meet and love yourself where you are at every turn of the page. You're brilliant and magical and you've got this!

Plotting a new course

Alright, Queens, here we are, at the final chunk of the present section of the book. This is exciting, isn't it? I mean, it is for me! We're at the point where we get to chart a course to our new lives. How we're going to implement the work we've done and by what time. You see, this bitch LOVES a road trip, whether literally or figuratively. It gets my juices flowing and makes me feel alive. I'm the sort of person who thrives on change. For example, most people want to die when presented with having to move houses. Not me! I'm itching to get the colored Sharpies out, make lists, get the packing tape and paper ready, and start to declutter physically and emotionally. And road trips get me just as high as moving does, I'm not going to lie. Something about the freedom of having nothing else to do but get your ass from point A to point B feels like a luxury in this go-go world. It's almost meditative looking into the future as the past falls away in your rearview mirror. And that's the stage we are at in your journey to your new life with you as an active and awake participant in it, rather than a "trauma zombie" going through the motions of a life you didn't even create with knowledge or consent.

So far the bulk of your life has likely been happenstance, reactionary to what you endured that caused you trauma. Listen, I'm no expert and I have no degrees. I only know that if I can get to the point where I am fully actively living and participating in my life, then surely some of the stuff that worked for me has got to help you. And isn't that what life is supposed to be all about: *Love your neighbors* in the same way you do yourself and *treat people the way you want them to treat you.* Super simple and easy to do, believe it or not. I'm always stunned by how many people can't seem to do these two little things. But I digress . . . I've gotten to a place of healing and now have a life that is completely and entirely worth living, whereas before I couldn't say that with confidence and faith.

Let's put the pedal to the metal and get you into the same place of contentment.

Are you ready to plot your new life path?

Hell, yeah! Of course you are! Here are some things to remember:

1.   Just fucking do it!

No, I'm not kidding. I'm dead serious. No more procrastinating. Those days of excuses, blaming, hiding, and responsibility shifting are long behind you. It's go time. Not tomorrow. Today. Remember what I said about tomorrow, and you don't need to look any further than your own life and how it dramatically shifted when you got locked in your home by a virus. There is no more time to waste. The luxury of assuming that you will have tomorrow and that there will be a "right" time are over. That entire notion of putting things off because you have lots of time in the future is a fallacy, a lie we're told—and tell ourselves—so we will overthink before we act. The reality of waiting for the perfect time or until you have the nerve to change your life will cause you to fall into the very real trap of never. Never doing it. Never having the time because you never made the time.

2. You are your greatest priority.

This is likely contrary to everything your parents ever told you about being a "good little person," but it's true, you are. There is nobody, not one single other person on this planet who is going to put your needs, your desires, or your dreams as their priority. No matter how much they love you. And please, let's have cooler heads prevail here, shall we? Other people NOT putting your dreams, aspirations, and wants as their priority does not mean they do not LOVE you. So, don't get in a fight with your person after reading this section and say, "Shantelle says you'll never honor my wants and dreams as your priority." Like they're the shittiest partner ever. The only person who owes you putting your desires first in their life is YOU. Stop waiting for somebody else to make your life a dream. You are the conductor of your own life, so get off your ass and go after it!

Disclaimer: I don't need anybody taking what I'm saying here as a

You are
your own
cheerleader,
your own hero,
your own
champion,
and your own
savior. Stop
waiting for
somebody else
to be all those
things for you.

license to become a narcissistic spawn of Satan. Honoring yourself and maximizing your one life to make it everything you want doesn't mean you trample on those around you to get it. I'm not saying become a C U Next Tuesday toward your loved ones or neglect them to finally realize your dreams. I'm saying that only you can shit or get off the pot and go after the life you want. So do it, but kindly.

You are your own cheerleader, your own hero, your own champion, and your own savior. Stop waiting for somebody else to be all those things for you.

3.   Give yourself hard deadlines.

No pussy footing around taking action. If you know you need to get a new job, then give yourself a cutoff date to be out of your current job. For example, if you have holiday time in the bank with your current employer, instead of using that time to lie on your couch scrolling through your phone or going to the Caribbean, use that time to secure interviews with potential new employers. And as you do this particular exercise of searching for your new dream job, remember that you didn't come this far to make lateral life moves. You came this far to be at the point where you're ready to make MASSIVE LIFE-CHANGING MOVES. This same principle applies if you're getting out of a relationship that you know you should not be in. Set a date. And share that with a friend you know will 1,000 percent hold you to your word. Because let's not lie to one another—we've come too far in our relationship to do that now—it's too damn easy to break promises to ourselves. I know it cuz I'm guilty as hell for doing it.

4.   Move forward.

This is the final direction that I'm going to give to assist you in carving your new path in this beautiful thing called life. Go to the section of your journal where you've completed all the exercises and prompts from this book and tear them out. Now get a stainless steel bowl and matches and take those pages to your outdoor space. Ball up each page filled with your past, your torment, and your pain, and place it in the bowl. After you've done this, light the pages, close your eyes, and say, "I am released from your hold on me. I am free. I let it be, and so it is."

Actually, I lied, there is one final thing you need to do in order to successfully move forward into your future—love yourself wholly and completely.

Love yourself without limits.

Love yourself without judgment.

Love yourself without censorship.

Love yourself and be loved in return.

YOUR
FUTURE

Looking for love in all the RIGHT places!

This is the GOOD STUFF RIGHT HERE! I love plotting, dreaming, and scheming for my future. It is literally one of the things that brings me the most joy. Yannick and I will talk for hours *ad nauseam* about what our next house will be like: where it will be, what the architecture of it will be, what colors the exterior will be, and how will we furnish it. It is fun for me and us. I love imagining a brighter, bigger, more robust future than what I'm currently living in. It's not as a fuck you to my present. It's not because I'm unhappy or ungrateful with where I'm at in my beautiful, full life. It's more as a way to stay on task of ensuring that I don't ever stop dreaming or aspiring for more, or working hard, working smart, and planning for the rest of my days.

I know what you're probably thinking: "But wait, way back at the beginning of this book you told me in no uncertain terms that I need to live in the present. I need to not take today for granted because there is no promise of tomorrow, and now you're saying that you're obsessed with living in your future? Say what?"

Yeah. That's right, true, and accurate.

But I can happily and joyfully create my future because I am currently fully and wholly living in my present. And I'm living every single day to its fullest. I am that bitch who will be sliding into my grave saying, "That was one hell of a ride!" I won't ever stop envisioning my future successes—and you shouldn't either. It's called drive. It's called ambition. It's called inspiration, and it's what gets you out of bed in the morning. Unless you have a two-year-old, then I have to say that it is definitely the two-year-old who is getting you out of bed each and every morning!

Listen to me, my beautiful bodacious friends. You have to fill your days with love. Love of self. Love of today and love for your future. If you have no vision for where you want to be in one, five, or ten years, then you likely will lack direction. And I don't know about you, but when I lack direction, I get into trouble. Both emotionally and physically. I operate much, much better when I'm working off a game plan. Usually it's in my head, rarely on paper because I am a Gemini and I sort of like to go where the wind blows me. Or where I see shiny things.

Your Call to Action

Exercise: Now that we've done so much work, I think the best thing to do now is create a road map, on paper (even though I just totally admitted to you that it's usually not my jam) in order for you to see where there are love holes in your life. Open your *WLYC* journal to a fresh new page. Reflect on these questions and write down your answers without overthinking them. Let your answers flow.

- What does love look like to you?
- What does love feel like to you?
- What color is love?
- What areas do you find you're missing or lacking love in your life?
- What does self-love look like to you?
- What does intimate and deep love feel like to you?

- Are you currently getting the love that feeds your soul in your friendships? With your parents (if they're both still alive)? And in your primary intimate relationship?

Take your time with this exercise. So many of us who are wounded don't even know where to begin to ask for love or how to cultivate love within ourselves, so this exercise, although it seems quite straightforward, might be quite difficult for you to put into words.

What does looking for love in all the right places look like? Where does one start? Well, first, you have to turn your gaze inward. Not in a navel gazing picking lint out of your belly button way, but in a very real and honest assessment of what love looks and feels like to you.

That's why we started this section with this exercise. It's truly important to this next step, so I encourage you to put this book aside until you can complete it. If it's not completed, you're not going to be able to do what's coming up next because you will not have identified within your own soul what love looks like to you. When you have done it, jump right back in because this next section is fun and juicy!

Making sure you're getting the love you need in this one life of yours depends totally and entirely on you. If you don't love and stand in your own worth, ain't nobody else going to do it either. And this is sadly the damn truth about being human. The way you treat yourself teaches others how to love, honor, cherish, and treat you. You set the bar for every other relationship in your life. So, from this day forward my, badass lionesses, you are not going to except any half-truth love. Not from yourself. Not

> The way you treat yourself teaches others how to love, honor, cherish, and treat you. You set the bar for every other relationship in your life.

from anybody else. That shit is in the past. You left that behind with all the other trauma, wounds, pain, and nonsense. This is your FUTURE. This is how your life is going to go for the rest of your life, so set yourself up for the life you deserve as a perfect child of God.

The way I was able to start receiving the love I deserved was by setting standards and expectations in how I was going to show up for myself in all the ways I'm going to list.

Your Call to Action

Exercise: If you see an area of weakness in the following list, you will know that that's an area inside of you that needs to be fortified by your newfound way to create boundaries. I've included some questions for you to answer to help bring clarity. Let's explore these points together!

Speaking my truth. Alright, this surprisingly always came easy to me. I was never one to hold back anything at all. What I did lack, however, was decorum around how I delivered my truth. Obviously, it's not a great thing to not be able to communicate clearly and calmly. It took me having a strong, loving, and gentle partner with impeccable communication skills to help me hone my way of sharing my truth that was more pleasant for others to receive.

- How are you at speaking your truth?
- Do you do it firmly, clearly, and respectfully?
- Do you even have emotional access to your truth?

Standing up for myself. This essentially goes hand in hand with standing in my truth, although it took me quite some time to be able to stand up for myself because I was afraid that would hurt people around me. I didn't realize that advocating for myself and establishing firm emotional parameters was a key part to me loving and honoring myself. This was something I had to really work at. Pointing out when I felt like I was being wronged by others and articulating what it was I needed from them in order to feel seen, heard, and respected was hard for me. I also needed to learn to stand up for myself as a woman in business because I was afraid of being called an emotional or difficult bitch if I was firm or demanding. If any of you reading this are in business for yourself, then you're bound to understand. For the first little while in business, I found

I was tiptoeing around issues with male business owners and not standing up for myself in the areas and during the times that I needed to.

- How are you at standing up for yourself?
- Is protecting yourself in this way emotionally available to you?
- If not what do you think you need to do to change it?

Listening to my inner voice. For the longest time I couldn't even hear my inner voice. She was so muted by all the muck and upset of the past. I didn't pay attention to what she was trying to tell me because I had spent so many years pushing her down and silencing her in order to protect others around me who I loved. It took some time to let her back to the surface to help me move forward by making choices that were based on her guidance. Some people call it your inner voice, your instinct, your gut.

- Whatever you call her, how is your relationship with her?
- Are you in a strong relationship with her?
- And if not, how can you call her back to you?

Trusting my inner voice. Obviously, in order to trust her, I had to release her. Once I got back into communication with her and was listening to her again, I took the time to reflect back on all the ways that ignoring her had not served me. I then compared those moments in my life to the times when I did pay attention to her and let her guide me. When I was able to compare the two, it was a no-brainer that I needed to trust her. I could see that she loved me and was extremely knowledgeable at not only keeping me safe, but also about what I needed to have peace and voice in my life.

- Do you trust your inner voice?
- In what ways has she protected and served you?

Honoring my inner voice. The best way I know how to honor my inner voice is to listen to and respect that bitch! Which I do more and more of. I now call on her whenever I sit down to write. Before I need to have a difficult conversation, I ask her to take over me. I ask her to steer and guide me in a way that will lighten my load. And I always, always thank her for being with me through the good, the bad, and the ugly, for never leaving me, even when I had abandoned her.

- How are you honoring your inner voice?

Making decisions based on what feels real, true, right, and best for me. This one is such a hot potato topic right now in our current world climate. Not very long ago, in fact, just over two years ago, nobody really cared what you did with your body. I mean other than the militant pro-lifers and anti-LGBTQ+ people, the general vibe was: "You do you as long as it doesn't affect me." But then we had a pandemic, a highly infectious virus running rampant and we were all scared. We were all taken aback and willing to do what it took in those first weeks and months to protect those around us. Then slowly over time, those who were in excellent health and trusted their bodies somehow became the enemy. I personally like to blame the mainstream media for this divisive work. And our "live and let live" mantra went by the wayside, and vitriol and hatred toward those who didn't share our beliefs became the norm. I respect and appreciate how much more difficult it has been to make decisions that are based on your own critical thinking, that feel good, right, true, and best for you during these last two years. For so many, the pandemic made us feel confused, isolated, and angry, regardless of what side of this particular global matter you are on. It has not been easy for anybody. But I'm here to tell you that at the end of the day, the only person you're ultimately going to be left with is you. Parents will sadly pass, lovers will too, and children will move on to their own lives. To love yourself, really love yourself, you must hold on and make choices that ultimately you can feel good about one, two, ten years down the road. And everybody else, well, they can make the decisions that feel good, right, true, and best for them.

- Do you find it easy or difficult to make and hold to decisions that feel best for you?

- Are you easily swayed by peers and others to be knocked off your truth?

Standing in my truth. These also go hand in hand; you cannot have one without the other. You have to bring to light what it is that matters to you, what feels real, true, right, and best for you. Some of us might not even have access to what this is because it's been shut off for so long. Maybe you were told you were stupid or incapable, so you never determined what any of this looks like in your life. Well, to find love flourishing inside of yourself, you have to get down to business and reveal what matters to you in life. When we know our truth, we're much more likely to disassociate ourselves from people whose views are in stark contrast to ours, such as racists. We might need to remove passively aggressive friends who try to bully us into their way of thinking. Once you uncover this stuff, it will be a hell of a lot easier to stand in your truth!

- Find the moral, political, and social issues that matter to you.
- Make a list of people who don't align with what you really think, believe, or feel.
- Decide if and when you can discuss these issues with them, or if it's time to call it quits with them.

Holding my boundaries. Again, these self-love rules of engagement all roll into one another. For me, I always found it difficult to not only hold, but to establish boundaries with people I perceived to be "above" me. I so desperately wanted to be liked and accepted that I allowed myself to become like them so they'd want to do business with me or hang out with me or help me in my own endeavors. It took me a long time to realize that nothing built on a slippery slope of sand can last. So I began to not only create boundaries in my life with everybody in my life, but I also honored and held them up. A book that really started me on this true path of boundary building was *Year of Yes* by Shonda Rhimes. Her book opened my eyes to my own power and my damn right to own my power.

- We discussed boundaries earlier; how are you doing with holding yours?
- Are there areas where you need to shore up the foundation?
- Are there relationships where you still haven't implemented them and you're feeling not great because of it?
- If yes, when and how are you going to stop screwing around and set those damn boundaries?

Sharing my needs and wants with the people I'm in relationships with. I was such a people pleaser, MY GOD. Which was weird cuz on the one hand I was spicy, speaking my truth and standing my ground, while having zero ability to ask for what I wanted. I remember when I was little I hated hearing the word "no," so I quickly stopped asking direct questions of my parents. I became a master avoider of asking direct questions. Seemed like a good idea at the time, until it wasn't. Until I realized that I was not getting a single one of my needs met because I didn't have the ability to simply ask for it, come what may: yes, no, or fuck off. It took a huge amount of work for me to get to the point where I could ask for what I wanted and needed. In fact, in full best friend transparency, I often slide back into being that little girl who doesn't ask for what she needs, who ends up hurt, angry, and disappointed when the people in my life fail to be mind readers and just magically know what emotional or physical gift to provide me with.

- Are you being clear in your communication of asking for what you need and want with those in your life?

Admitting my weaknesses. Oh, baby! This was another difficult one to let others see. I mean, think about it. Anytime I was vulnerable (or weak), bad things happened to me. So it became super, super important to my survival to NOT show any sign of weakness. Newsflash, in case you haven't experienced this yourself, if you don't allow others to see you when you're weak, in need, and vulnerable, they're never going to be able to support, comfort, or love you through it.

- Start admitting your weaknesses to those who you trust will hold the space for you to do so and who will always protect you while you are in a state of vulnerability.

It is not irresponsible to make yourself a priority—it is actually RESPONSIBLE.

Asking for support. Asking for what you want and need is not the same as asking for support. Asking for support is asking for help, for reinforcement, for strength. It means to not go it alone.

- What are some areas in your life where you could ask for support?

Prioritizing my needs, wants, and desires. Once you come to see what support you need and in what areas of your life it's needed, and you understand the importance of communicating clearly what it is you must have in this life to feel loved, it becomes much easier to prioritize your needs, wants, and desires. The largest challenge for most of us (yes, I have my hand up here) is to stay consistent in making sure these things are being met, first by yourself and within yourself, and then obviously your relationships outside the one you have with you! I for one am extremely jealous of my husband and how he has been able to make sure that he prioritizes things that feed his soul, without fail or interruption. He makes sure he spends hours and hours in nature, either by building bike trails or riding them. He knows that spending time with Mother Earth reconnects him to himself and enables him to be a better human and partner. Most men are extremely good at this. Hello, golf, anyone? Or how about Sunday football. Men never apologize for prioritizing themselves, and yet us women (yes, my hand is up WAY HIGH again), not only apologize for it, but in fact, will often spend years not doing it at all. Not anymore. It is not irresponsible to make yourself a priority—it is actually RESPONSIBLE.

- How are you ensuring that you're keeping yourself a priority?
- What daily rituals or activities do you participate in that help you to have your needs and desires met?

Letting myself live without judgment. As a recovering bulimic, it has been a long, difficult, and painful journey to be able to look in the mirror without passing judgment on myself. It has also been incredibly hard to eat without attaching negative, hateful speech to what I put in my mouth. I'd love to sit here and type that I have totally healed all this, but sadly, I have not. I can, however, say that I've made huge strides thanks to the fucking kick-ass book *The F*ck It Diet* that I mentioned earlier. If you're struggling with eating issues and are constantly yo-yo dieting, hating food while simultaneously obsessing over it, then I strongly, vehemently advise you to go and get this book!

- How do you live in judgment of yourself?
- And how has this served you?
- When are you willing to let this go?

Aging in a way that feels beautiful to me. This topic is another doozy! So many people get so fucking mad at people who "don't age naturally." In fact, it's a huge, huge thing on social media right now to shame women who like to age a little more gradually, like me, than go to sleep one day looking like themselves and wake up the next day looking like their fathers, which was also me. I'm not afraid of wrinkles; I just don't want to look like I hate the world . . . even though some days . . . but I digress. The bottom line is YOU DO YOU. If you have the means and you want injections, whose business is it anyway? If you want to color your hair, do it. I've recently decided to let my gray come in, and I'm not mad about it. I am a grandmother, after all. But this is not about me. It is really nobody's business how you age but yours. I mean there's a reason that the beauty industry raked in $511 billion dollars in 2021, and that was with most of us stuck in our houses! We want to feel pretty and look pretty, and that should be OKAY. But for some people, it really isn't. To them I say, "Just mind your damn business!"

Exploring interests

My friends, I cannot express enough how crucial this is to your healing, your growth, and your emotional fulfillment to find things that interest you! Like really interest you. If I hadn't experienced it in my own life, then I wouldn't be out here yelling from the rooftops: EXPLORE YOUR INTERESTS! It develops character, it builds confidence if said interest is something that requires that you develop a new skill. It helps with self-esteem; and let's be frank, the more things we know how to do, the more interesting we are—to ourselves and to others. And there's no shame in being your most interesting self!

I've shared with you some of the things I've been doing these last few years that used to interest me from afar, skills that others had developed within themselves that I admired, such as horseback riding, wakeboarding, wake surfing, and writing books to name a few. I still have a lengthy list of things to try, like surfing, painting, learning to play the piano, golf, and tennis. I won't rest until all my current interests have been attempted, and by then, I'm confident I will have added more to my list. I encourage you to make a list of things that interest you, and there's no better place to create that exciting list than in your very own *WLYC* journal! Take a few minutes right now to write it out.

Doing things that scare me

This was huge for me, because as I've shared throughout this book, I had a lot of beliefs and fears about doing scary things that kept me from trying them. But as I slowly began to do more of the stuff that freaked me out, the braver I became. It builds trust and faith when you do things that frighten you. And when you get to the other side and you're still alive, you start to have more belief that the world is a safe place for you to reside in, which in turn allows you to live more wholly and freely in it. It really is that straightforward. If there is shit in your life that scares you, and you know within your heart of hearts that it is an unjust fear, then I suggest you make a plan to meet that fear head on. I happen to have a fear of skydiving, and no matter how many people take to a plane and throw themselves to the ground from 18,000 feet (something my hubby and two of our daughters did together), I can assure you that this bitch will never do that. Know your limits and break your fears in a way that makes sense and feels right to you. Because remember what scares you might not scare me, and vice versa! They're your fears and they're yours to overcome. You're not in competition with anybody to break through them, and nobody even needs to know that you've taken this on. So, what are you waiting for? Write down your "scares the shit out of me list," then get to crossing those things off one by one!

Staying the new improved course

I tell this to anybody who will actually listen to me. You want to feel really good about yourself and have a healthy future? Limit, or hell, eliminate all together, your time on social media. Stop comparing yourself to everybody else you see on there. We all know that everybody is only showcasing their highlight reels! Actually, let me back up a step. This is no longer true. Now, the huge trend on Instagram is to show everybody how flawed you are. The new badge of honor is to let everybody observe your stretch marks, your belly folds, and the like. And I have to say, I'm really here for it. I am. Love everybody and love every body. There is not one way for a body to be beautiful or healthy or strong. I'm totally behind this message, like 1,000,000 percent behind this. But—and it's a big but—when people have pages like this as just another way to establish brand or fame, it kind of feels gross to me. It really doesn't seem that

> Love everybody and love every body. There is not one way for a body to be beautiful or healthy or strong.

different than the calculated, staged photos of the perfect life. I mean, it's the same curated shit just packaged in different wrapping. Doesn't it make you feel bad if you are somebody without belly rolls cuz you're naturally thin? Do these sites and "influencers" not still profit from and get wealthy off the same notion of body shaming women for financial gain? I mean it seems like it to me. So, now we are being inundated by this new wave of "body positivity" and are being told to love our bodies exactly as they are, which is a good thing, right? Well, not so fast. We can't simply follow somebody who seemingly has cracked the self-loathing, shame affair we've likely been battling for most if not all of our lives because somebody on Instagram has done so. We need to do a whole whack of work to get to the place where we're ready to even acknowledge that there is possibility of healing in this area. And for me, what I discovered was that once I had gone all the way back to the root of my self-hatred, it became significantly easier for me to make up my own damn mind about what mattered to me. What weight felt best for me, for all the right reasons. Am I strong at this weight? Am I healthy? Is my blood pressure good? Are my cholesterol and sugar levels low? Once I was able to love myself in earnest, I was able to unravel the lies around what my body should weigh, look like, and be able to do. Still, this bitch has not given up on trying to be able to do a handstand! I do honor my body for where she is at, not where somebody else is on the internet.

If you're not going to get off social media all together, then might I

This for me is the perfect way to bookend a day: begin it with intention and end it in gratitude.

persuade you to do a full gut job of who you are spending your days with. Now that you've done all this work and uncovered what really matters to you and what is important to feeding your soul and loving yourself, my guess is that this will come easily. And in fact, you might be way ahead of me and this call to action might have taken place way back in the severing of ties. But if it hasn't, and it's the one remaining sticky icky part of your daily life, then do it now.

Another way I'm able to stay my course of self-love and honoring of my spirit is by doing one thing a day that is just for me. It might mean spending some time in nature or doing yoga or working out with weights. It could be a lunch or dinner date with a friend or picking up the phone and having an actual chat with somebody I'm missing and want to connect with. I do this every single day, along with daily reading and meditation. Before getting out of bed, I ask my inner voice what it is I need from today. I communicate to and with myself so that I'm sure that I'm not hitting the ground running already disconnected from myself. When we're not connected to ourselves it's so much easier to deny yourself what it is you need to have a good day. Therefore, take the time to think about what sort of day you want to have before you start your day. I usually pair this with the ritual of listing five things I'm grateful for before I fall asleep. This for me is the perfect way to bookend a day: begin it with intention and end it in gratitude.

Remember, you're still only one person. You have healed shit, but you haven't built a bionic woman! Have grace with yourself. Eradicate keeping score. Stop measuring your life against anybody else's, and stop putting yourself down for not accomplishing something by a self-imposed time-line, especially if you're comparing your journey and timeline to someone else's. You are not in competition with anybody. Not even with yourself.

You are in a state of self-love and honoring you, but that doesn't mean you've got a license to lie on your couch eating bonbons. No. I'm simply trying to get you to shift your mindset from being goal oriented to being soul oriented. You will achieve that if you come at it with love and from love. Trust me. I'm also going to need you to be understanding and patient with yourself. You will fall back into old habits and patterns, and it's not the end of the world. You will get overwhelmed and feel hopeless from time to time, although like me, I hope this sense of dread and hopelessness becomes less and less frequent to the point where it is a long forgotten piece of you. Some days, you will want to take a break. You'll want to rest and just stop. That's totally okay. Rest. But don't stop, don't quit. You're still

> . . . shift your mindset from being goal oriented to being soul oriented.

going to face challenges, you're still going to be triggered, and you're still going to be living in the world and dealing with life. Some days will be so much harder than others, but you've come too far to give up on yourself. It is not an option ever again to abandon yourself. Stay the course, and always remember that you are not alone. You have an entire pride of other lionesses beside and behind you. Build that circle, build your pride, lean on them when it gets too heavy, and ask for support. Life is not meant to be lived alone, so call on your people when it gets dark and difficult. We've got you!

You might get discouraged because change isn't happening fast enough. I get it. I feel that too, and often. But the real truth is that you have changed so much. You have slayed demons while reading this book and being on this journey with me. You have overcome massive emotional obstacles and knocked down walls that made you a prisoner of your own life. You have done amazing work! You are a force to be reckoned with, and you are beautiful and magical. You are a perfect wonderful child of God—don't you ever forget it.

Making sure the good shit rolls
downhill

Alright, badass Queens, here we are, at the end of this portion of our journey together. Although I do hope that you will continue the conversations with me on Instagram and through my website. My hope and prayer for each and every one of you glorious, perfect beings is that you will have found some solace in my words. That you feel understood, seen, heard, and supported. Often times, it's the fear that we're out here all alone and that we're the only person who has had the experience that we've had that keeps us stuck in upset. But the reality is that even though the negative experience that we've each had is completely unique to us, the way that it landed in our body, heart, and soul, how we process it, and how it manifests in our life is not. Bodies work the way they do, and how intense pain is stored in the cells is the same for you as it is for me. And this is how we are alike. It's because of the shared result of trauma that we can relate to one another.

I realized the extent of my trauma once life slowed down for me. I spent so long running around with three busy daughters, with each of them trying out different activities in an attempt to find one that sparked their joy and passion. Once they were able to do homework on their own, have playdates, sleepovers, and "bigger kid" life stuff, when they began to need me less, my trauma emerged from the deep dark cavern I had stuffed it into. It wasn't until a brilliant therapist enlightened me that my trauma reared its ugly head when my girls were becoming the age that I was when all my abuse started. Our cells have memory, and it was on a cellular level that I was reliving my traumatic childhood when my girls were between the ages of nine and fifteen. It was then that the wheels really came off my train, let me tell you. And because I didn't understand what was going on inside of me, I took my pain out on everybody around me. But mostly me. I was making bad decision after bad decision. I was lashing out at the world at large, but mostly I was destroying myself. It wasn't until years later while doing this healing work that I came to the brutal and painful realization that while I was not cleared of my past childhood wounds, I in turn did as you can expect and assume, and caused trauma in my own beautiful, perfect, innocent girls. Unwittingly. Without forethought or malice, I leaked my raw wounds all over them.

You don't want to be like me. If you're a momma, I hope I'm catching you before you, too, unknowingly share your intergenerational trauma with your unsuspecting and wholesome offspring. A book I loved that truly helped me understand how deep familial trauma can go is *Black Girl in Love (With Herself)* written by a force of nature, Trey Anthony. If I can encourage you to buy one more book during our time together,

I would love it if you grabbed this one, especially if this cycle sounds familiar to you.

You see we cannot hold ourselves to the fire for how we behave toward others when we're still unknowing about what it is inside of us that needs to be undone for us to be our best selves. We cannot, but we still do. Remember, my lovelies, if we punish ourselves and hold regret in our hearts, then we're perpetuating the cycle of not forgiving and keeping ourselves in a toxic prison of shame. We cannot love freely when we're consumed with our own shortcomings, when we're so focused on ourselves and living in a pity party for one. You must keep your eyes up and looking out. Healing is not a one and done project. It takes your daily commitment to putting in the work for it to exist. Before I knew where my character blind spots were, I'd often get triggered. Even now, from time to time, I sometimes slip back into old habits, old patterns of being. Sometimes I get triggered by something that my husband or one of my girls says or does, and I'm not always refined or dignified in how I share my upset with them. Now, I could give you a whole list of why I let my shit run downhill, like lack of sleep, they were shitty to me first . . . blah-blah-blah. Who cares. The end result was that I didn't maintain my level of communication integrity in a situation that I knew was going to push my buttons, and I reverted back to my wounded child with my fists up. So I end up saying "I'm sorry" a lot. I end up having to humble out and own my shit. I need to remove the harsh word vomit from their shoulders, hearts, and spirits, and let them know that the negative outburst was all mine. That I was taking my emotional agony out on them.

It's nobody's fault when you react in a way that is unkind. It is yours, so own it.

When you stand in the middle of a conflict that you're participating in, and you are able to catch hold of your emotional self and recognize that you are fighting in an undignified and disrespectful way, you stop your shit from rolling downhill in rock star fashion. When we're tuned in to ourselves and are able to catch ourselves in this way, we teach others that there is another way to have conflict, a better way to have conflict, and a powerful and peaceful way to work out conflict.

During a disagreement or fight, my very real issue that I still default to as words are coming out of my mouth, my brain is saying, "I know better than to ____." But in the heat of the moment of a "perceived battle" mixed with a healthy heaping of ego, look out. It's like my shit faucet got stuck on. This is something that I am currently STILL working on, catching myself while I'm in the heated moment of self-defense. It has to do with my flight or fight switch going on whenever conflict is happening, because when I was young and my dad was fighting, it meant somebody was getting smacked around. We're all onions with so many layers, and so often when we're having a setback—which we will have because, hello, we're still a human having a human experience with many other humans, who may or may not have healed their own traumas—we're going to get triggered. You're going to fall back into a defensive, sympathetic mode. Remember you lived there for so long, so you will often find your way back there more organically than fighting with elegance and maturity. You'll likely end up there when you're trying really, really hard to NOT end up there. You are human, after all.

Remember that. Don't spiral into shamedom. Don't think you're failing at being your recovered self and throw in the towel and take up residency in "I Give Up Ville." Acknowledge that you've slipped. It's common to repeat what you've learned, how you've learned to protect yourself for so long, and to default to that when you feel threatened. So, when you speak aggressively or you name call or speak cruelly when you're hurt—STOP. Like, literally stop. Stop talking. Regroup. And regrouping might mean that you need to remove yourself from the conflict, from the upset, from the thing that is triggering you and pulling you backward into your old coping patterns. Call a time-out on the heated situation. Go pray. Meditate. Punch a pillow. Dance it out. Do whatever works to calm you down. Once you're calm, get back into the conversation and hopefully bring it to a resolution.

You've got this. You've done such amazing, brave work. Stay the course. Continue moving forward with your new healthy habits, joys, and passions that you have now uncovered. A most important piece of the puzzle to ensure that you keep moving away from your trauma is to keep your life focused on these joys. Continue to live in the space of being "done with it." So often we believe, or assume, that the only way to truly stop being in trauma is to relive it, to rehash it, to keep picking at it, but that's not the way at all. To keep the shit from running downhill for the rest of your days is to make sure that you are fully and entirely committed to living a life of pleasure. Remind yourself every single day that you are worthy of a peaceful life. Make sure to start your day with something that is pleasurable for you. Don't feel guilty about doing something only for you when you open your eyes. Get in touch with yourself and uncover what activity would bring you joy to participate in before you had to commit yourself to your adulthood and your "reality" of job, family, or whatever your daily obligations are. Expose what this is for you, then make it your ritual. It might be waking up to a quiet house and sipping coffee in your favorite chair while gazing out a window. It might be going for a run. It might be painting. I don't know what that is for you, but find the thing

> Remind yourself every single day that you are worthy of a peaceful life.

that you can implement into every single morning that starts you off connected to a place of contentment, satisfaction, and gratitude. When we are grounded in gratitude, it is so very difficult to focus on pain.

Something that I need to do often is to remind myself where I was a week ago, a month ago, a year ago. I'm a super A-type person who didn't stand in line when they were handing out patience. I want everything yesterday. I even came out of the womb twelve days early to get this party started! So I get what it's like when it feels like life isn't going anywhere for you. When you are 1,000 percent confident that you've

When we are grounded in gratitude, it is so very difficult to focus on pain.

made less than zero progress on continuing to move your life forward. Don't get discouraged if you still hit a fast food drive-through even though you said you would never do that again back in the severing ties to old habits section of this book. We all slip and fall. It's not the slipping and falling in life that is our problem, it's always going to be 1) how long do you stay there; and 2) do you throw in the towel completely? Keep yourself focused on how far you've come, not how far you still have to go.

It's so easy to punish yourself when you have a setback, but please promise me that you will be kind to yourself, that you will stop and look in the mirror and remind yourself that you are . . . what? Say it with me: I AM A HUMAN BEING HAVING A HUMAN EXPERI-ENCE. I AM NOT A ROBOT! Having a setback is a beautiful way to reexperience your growth because you're going to get mentally stronger and stronger each time. And the very thing that might have put you on your ass for a week, might now only take the wind out of your sails for an hour. Failing and falling down are opportunities for us to put all that we've learned into practice; it gives us the opportunity to use our tools that we've been collecting.

Finally, my fellow fierce lionesses, I want you to hold fast to the knowing that the best way to ensure that you keep your shit from rolling downhill is to constantly be on top of it. Just because you've done the work, doesn't mean that the work is done. For example, think of getting a haircut. One haircut doesn't mean your hair is going to keep that shape forever and ever, and neither is your healing. You won't just magically stay healed and run off into a glorious field of daises and butterflies. (Oh, but wouldn't that be grand if it did?) I mean, it wouldn't be for me because I get bored SO easily, but you get my point. You need to keep up with your healthy and positive habits to stay healthy and positive. You can't keep cigarettes lying around if you want to be successful at quitting smoking. The best way to ensure you continue on your new path of honoring and holding up all your hard work and efforts is to have structure in your life. To keep implementing the things that got you here in the first place, meditation, journaling, singing, whatever the positive things are that you replaced the negative destructive habits with. Remember to do these things every single day.

I have one final thing that I want you to do—be grateful. And if it isn't already a part of your daily rituals, please add it in because as I mentioned earlier, a life lived in deep gratitude leaves no room for anything else to reside. Not pain.

Not anger.

Not bitterness.

Not judgment.

Not lack.

Not revenge.

Not regret.

Nothing.

Your Call to Action

Exercise: Get into a comfortable position. Inhale deeply. Exhale fully.

Say this out loud:

I accept that the presence of gratitude fills my entire body, my cells, my soul.

I am grateful for my body.

I am grateful for my hands, arms, legs, eyes, ears, mouth, and heart.

I am grateful for my mind.

I am grateful that my body serves me and all the ways that it does.

I am grateful for every person in my life.

I am grateful for every single experience I have had in this life, the supposed bad and good.

I am grateful for the ways that these experiences have shaped, formed, and molded me.

I am grateful for yesterday and today.

I am grateful for the ways that I am strong.

I am grateful for the ways that I am soft.

I am grateful for the grace of God, the Divine that holds me up and carries me through my life journey.

I am grateful for all my joys and all my sorrows.

I am grateful for what I've lost and what I've gained.

I am grateful for love. To have the ability to love and to be loved.

I am gratitude.

Breathe in gratitude. Breathe out love. Breathe in gratitude. Breathe out love.

It is so, and so it is.

I am thankful to you and for you.

Keep rising, and remember to always keep your brilliant, bold, wonderful self facing the sun.

Love, *Shantelle*

ACKNOWLEDGMENTS

I'd like to first thank every single person who has crossed my path who didn't know that I was a beautiful shining child of God. That I was loved and protected by the Divine. That your acts committed against me only brought out the best in me: an abundance of kindness, generosity, a deep well of compassion and love for others who were abused. I absolutely forgive you with my whole heart and being because I truly understand that you did not know what you were doing. You were not taught, guided, or raised in a way to understand how to love others. You weren't taught to see, love, and honor their light. My prayer for each and every one of you is that you see it now. That you have also healed the dark corners in yourselves.

To my patient, kind, forgiving, and gentle husband, I'm sorry for the ways that my shit has run downhill onto you, onto your beautiful soft heart. The ways that my trauma and my belief that I was worthless caused me to treat you, all too often like you, too, were worthless. I'm blessed beyond my wildest dreams that you love me in spite of me. I'm grateful that you are on this journey with me and that you've had the stomach for thirty-four years now to never take my outbursts of pain personally. I love you, Yannick, and one lifetime will never ever be enough.

To all my therapists along the way, some who came in the form of trained educated professionals and others who showed up as friends, a sister-in-law, my three daughters, and colleagues. To all the people who played a part in me uncovering and healing the little girl in me, allowing her to step into a safe life overflowing with love, peace, and joy. Especially you, Leisse Wilcox. Damn. My work with you was the final piece in a very jagged jigsaw puzzle, and I will be eternally grateful for you for the rest of my days. Thank you, Queen.

To Sabrina Greer of YGTMedia for telling me to write this book when I thought there was no point after the first two—in my A-type, performance results-driven mind—"flopped." For encouraging me on every single front that my story needed to be told, shared, and sent out into the world. You never cease to amaze me with your ability to support, truly support, your burgeoning authors at all hours of the day and night. It's probably because you're an author first, publisher second. I don't just call you my publisher, but my friend. I'm profoundly thankful for the way you continue to assist me in bringing my whole vision of *Without*

Losing Your Cool to light. You're a force of nature, and I have mad, mad love for you.

Kelly Lamb, I'm stupid thankful for you coming in clutch at the eleventh hour. For spending a good amount of time researching my style by reading my other books and listening to my podcasts so you could be sure that you would "get my voice." And then working so diligently to keep it authentic throughout this entire book, which is so very important to me. You checked every step along the way to make sure that I felt that the writing of my healing journey was told in a way that felt real to me. You're amazing, and when I think of things I'm currently grateful for, you landing with this book on your desk is top of the list. Thank you, thank you, thank you.

The entire YGTMedia team: Christine Stock, for really fine tuning this one that is so close to my heart and was truly very difficult to put down on paper in a way that came across as I intended it to—as a book to heal me and others—and not complaining. Doris Chung, well, she's beautiful AGAIN! Thank you, thank you, thank you.

Erin Dean Williams, lady. Big, big, big love and respect for you and your incredible talents. Thank YOU for getting what I was going for with the look and feel of my brand *Without Losing Your Cool*. The colors, the fonts, the vibe is so perfect, and I truly couldn't be happier every single time I look at what you created for me. You rock!

Michelle Fairbanks. Wow. Just WOW. Your brilliant mind and your creative talents are deeply appreciated by me. The crazy awesome work you did to take what Erin created and run with it to round out the look and vibe of my brand, all my *Love Note* cards, and my two books with YGT has blown my mind. Everything is so fucking beautiful, I can't STAND IT! I am crazy proud to see my name on all of your designs.

Wendy Vincent for helping me pull up my bootstraps and encouraging me to write when I thought writing was over for me. You're a Queen in every sense of the word. Thank you.

My mom, honestly, I hope you know how incredibly strong you are. I love you completely, and I'm truly thankful it's you and me. And even though you likely should have given your kids away when you were just a kid yourself, I can't express to you enough how thankful I am you didn't. I love you, Mom.

For all of you who bought, shared, and read this book, I pray that whatever was in you that was holding you back and that caused you to live, play, and be small has been brought into the light, out of the shadows of your being, so you can live the whole, beautiful, magical life you deserve and are destined for. You have one life—spend every breathing moment living it, not simply getting through it. I believe in you. I've got you.

Last but never least, my girls, Brianna, Dominique, and Mikaela, thank you for helping me bring all my dreams of how and what I want

Without Losing Your Cool to be. And thank you mostly for being forgiving, compassionate, and patient with me as I raised you while simultaneously figuring out and raising me too. You bring me such joy, and you make all the fighting to uncover the best of myself worth it. I love you with every fiber of my being and look forward to all the shared experiences we're yet to enjoy together.

With love and gratitude,

xx Shantelle

RESOURCES

(in alphabetical order)

Books:

- *Black Girl in Love (With Herself)* Trey Anthony (Hay House, 2021)
- *Do the Work* Gary John Bishop (HarperOne, 2019)
- *Let That Sh*t Go* Nina Purewal (Collins, 2019)
- *Mating in Captivity* Esther Perel (Harper Paperbacks, 2006)
- *Stop Doing That Sh*t* Gary John Bishop (HarperOne, 2019)
- *The Body Is Not an Apology* Sonya Renee Taylor (Berrett-Koehler Publishers, 2018)
- *The Body Keeps the Score* Bessel Van der Kolk (Penguin Books, 2014)
- *The 5 Love Languages* Gary Chapman (Northfield Publishing, 2015)
- *The F*ck It Diet* Caroline Dooner (Harper Wave, 2019)
- *The State of Affairs* Esther Perel (Harper Paperbacks, 2017)
- *To Call Myself Beloved* Leisse Wilcox (YGTMedia Co., 2020)
- *Unfu*k Yourself* Gary John Bishop (HarperOne, 2016)

- *What Happened to You* Bruce D. Perry and Oprah Winfrey (Flatiron Books, 2021)
- *Wise as Fu*k* Gary John Bishop (HarperOne, 2020)
- *Year of Yes* Shonda Rhimes (Simon & Schuster, 2015)

Meditations:

- Giovanni Dienstmann (specifically his course on "Letting Go of Regret")
- Linda Hall
- Iyanla Vanzant

Podcasts:

- *We Can Do Hard Things* Glennon Doyle
- *Where Should We Begin?* Esther Perel
- *Without Losing Your Cool* Shantelle Bisson
- *Fix My Life* Iyanla Vanzant
- *On Purpose* Jay Shetty

Websites:

- www.biologyonline.com/
- www.caminorecovery.com/blog/how-trauma-manifests-on-a-cellular-level
- https://health.clevelandclinic.org/
- https://medium.com/@biobeats/how-unprocessed-trauma-is-stored-in-the-body-10222a76cbad
- www.nationalcac.org/wp-content/uploads/2016/08/HealthySexualDevelopmentOverview.pdf
- https://shantellebisson.com
- www.vitalityunleashed.com.au/cellular-memory-of-trauma

SHANTELLE BISSON

Two-time author Shantelle Bisson divides her time between Toronto, Los Angeles, and her marina, Shantilly's Place, in the Kawartha region of Ontario. In addition to being an author, producer, and recovering actress, Shantelle is mother to three beautiful daughters and two four-legged sons and is wife to Yannick Bisson, star of Canada's number one drama series, CBC's *Murdoch Mysteries*.

Shantelle believes strongly in giving back to the community. She sits on the committee of Childhood Cancer Canada and has cochaired their main fundraising event, The Purple Party, since 2012. Her involvement has helped raise more than $1.5 million to date. Shantelle also supports Bridgepoint Active Healthcare via their annual fundraiser, The Heist, as a donor. Additionally, Shantelle and her husband give generously to the APJ fund, supporting kids in Haiti by sponsoring their secondary school, and they sit on their Canadian Board as well as their Advisory Board. A childhood sexual abuse survivor, Shantelle joined forces with Boost for Kids as Honorary Chair, and she shared her story as the guest speaker at their 2018 Butterfly Ball. Shantelle's life has been centered around children since she became pregnant with her first daughter at nineteen, so it is no surprise that her charitable endeavors focus primarily on kids in need.

@shantellebisson

@withoutlosingyourcool

@shantellebisson

ShantelleBissonOfficial

www.shantellebisson.com

YGTMama Media Co. is a blended boutique publishing house for mission-driven humans. We help seasoned and emerging authors "birth their brain babies" through a supportive and collaborative approach. Specializing in narrative nonfiction and adult and children's empowerment books, we believe that words can change the world, and we intend to do so one book at a time.

🌐 www.ygtmama.com/publishing

🔘 @ygtmama.media.co

f @ygtmama.media.co

Made in the USA
Monee, IL
22 May 2022

96857272R00155